1st Workshop on Semiparametric Methods in NLP: Decoupling Logic from Knowledge (Spa-NLP 2022)

AA005145

Dublin, Ireland
27 May 2022

ISBN: 978-1-7138-6752-4

Printed from e-media with permission by:

Curran Associates, Inc.
57 Morehouse Lane
Red Hook, NY 12571

Some format issues inherent in the e-media version may also appear in this print version.

Copyright© (2022) by the Association for Computational Linguistics
All rights reserved.

Printed with permission by Curran Associates, Inc. (2023)

For permission requests, please contact the Association for Computational Linguistics at the address below.

Association for Computational Linguistics
209 N. Eighth Street
Stroudsburg, Pennsylvania 18360

Phone: 1-570-476-8006
Fax: 1-570-476-0860

acl@aclweb.org

Additional copies of this publication are available from:

Curran Associates, Inc.
57 Morehouse Lane
Red Hook, NY 12571 USA
Phone: 845-758-0400
Fax: 845-758-2633
Email: curran@proceedings.com
Web: www.proceedings.com

Spa-NLP 2022

The 1st Workshop on Semiparametric Methods in NLP: Decoupling Logic from Knowledge

Proceedings of the Workshop

May 27, 2022

The Spa-NLP organizers gratefully acknowledge the support from the following sponsors.

Gold

Meta

Silver

Google

Introduction

We are excited to present the inaugural workshop on semiparametric methods on NLP.
The field of natural language processing (NLP) has undergone a paradigm shift with the dramatic success of large pre-trained language models (LMs) on almost every downstream task. These large parametric models are based on the transformer architecture and are trained on massive collections of data using self-supervised learning, which are then fine-tuned on a relatively smaller set of task-specific supervised examples. The success of this simple recipe of homogeneous architectures and transfer learning has led to its widespread adoption.
Despite these successes, parametric models lack several desirable properties. For example, these models use knowledge stored in their parameters to perform tasks without providing provenance or transparency into the model mechanisms. This is further exacerbated when they make an erroneous prediction as it is challenging to understand what went wrong and how to fix it. Moreover, as new information arrives, existing knowledge becomes obsolete and should be updated. However, it is currently challenging to update the knowledge stored in the parameters of LMs. Amongst other issues, this has implications on personal privacy as we do not have a robust way to execute requests for deletion of personal information which could be stored in the parameters of the model.
Nonparametric instance-based models, on the other hand, offer many of the properties described above by design — a model capacity that naturally grows with data, easy addition and deletion of knowledge, and provenance for predictions based on the nearest neighbors with respect to the input. However, these models often suffer from weaker empirical performance compared to deep parametric models. Semi-parametric models are statistical models that consist of a fixed parametric and a flexible nonparametric component. Combining the advantages of both paradigms has the potential to remedy many of the short-comings described previously. For example, the nonparametric component can provide vast amounts of background knowledge and the parametric component can encode the logic required to solve the problem.
Recently, many recent works have independently proposed approaches that combine a parametric model with a nonparametric model in areas from question answering, language modeling, machine translation, and even protein structure prediction. Given the increasingly promising results on various tasks of such semiparametric models, we believe this area is ripe for targeted investigation on understanding efficiency, generalization, limitations, and to widen its applicability.
This workshop invited previously unpublished work as archival submissions, in addition to a non-archival track of previously-published work, recognising the fast-moving nature of this area, and the large amount of recently introduced work. After withdrawals, We have accepted a total of 5 archival papers, and 21 non-archival papers. Our final program thus includes 26 papers, 5 of which will be included in the proceedings.
We are excited to host six stellar invited speakers, who will each lend their perspective to this exciting and rapidly-evolving area. In the morning session, we will host Anna Potapenko, and in the afternoon session, we will host Danqi Chen, Jason Weston, Andrew McCallum and Hannaneh Hajishirzi. We shall finish with a panel discussion. We thank these speakers, our program committee, the ACL workshop chairs, and our sponsors, Google and Meta, for helping to make this workshop possible.

Non-Archival Papers

The following papers were submitted to our workshop as non-archival submissions.

- *Learning To Retrieve Prompts for In-Context Learning* Ohad Rubin, Jonathan Herzig, Jonathan Berant
- *A Survey of Knowledge-Intensive NLP with Pre-Trained Language Models* Da Yin, Li Dong, Hao Cheng, Xiaodong Liu, Kai-Wei Chang, Furu Wei, Jianfeng Gao
- *KNN-BERT: Fine-Tuning Pre-Trained Models with KNN Classifier* Linyang Li, Demin Song, Ruotian Ma, Xipeng Qiu, Xuanjing Huang
- *Learning to Retrieve Passages without Supervision* Ori Ram,Gal Shachaf,Omer Levy,Jonathan Berant,Amir Globerson
- *Hyperlink-induced Pre-training for Passage Retrieval in Open-domain Question Answering* Jiawei Zhou,Xiaoguang,Lifeng Shang,Lan Luo,Ke Zhan,Enrui Hu,Xinyu Zhang,Hao Jiang,Zhao Cao,Fan Yu,Xin Jiang,Qun Liu,Lei Chen
- *Towards Continual Knowledge Learning of Language Models* Joel Jang, Seonghyeon Ye, Sohee Yang, Joongbo Shin, Janghoon Han, Gyeonghun Kim, Stanley Jungkyu Choi, Minjoon Seo
- *Learning Cross-Lingual IR from an English Retriever* Yulong Li, Martin Franz, Md Arafat Sultan, Bhavani Iyer, Young-Suk Lee, Avirup Sil
- *C-MORE: Pretraining to Answer Open-Domain Questions by Consulting Millions of References* Xiang Yue, Xiaoman Pan, Wenlin Yao, Dian Yu, Dong Yu, Jianshu Chen
- *Towards Unsupervised Dense Information Retrieval with Contrastive Learning* Gautier Izacard, Mathilde Caron, Lucas Hosseini, Sebastian Riedel, Piotr Bojanowski, Armand Joulin, Edouard Grave
- *Internet-augmented language models through few-shot prompting for open-domain question answering* Angeliki Lazaridou, Elena Gribovskaya, Wojciech Stokowiec, Nikolai Grigorev
- *Towards Interactive Language Modeling* Maartje ter Hoeve, Evgeny Kharitonov, Dieuwke Hupkes, Emmanuel Dupoux
- *GUD-IR: Generative Retrieval for Semiparametric Models* Aman Madaan, Niket Tandon, Peter Clark, Yiming Yang
- *Less is More: Summary of Long Instructions is Better for Program Synthesis* Kirby Kuznia, Swaroop Mishra, Mihir Parmar, Chitta Baral
- *How Many Data Samples is an Additional Instruction Worth?* Ravsehaj Singh Puri, Swaroop Mishra, Mihir Parmar, Chitta Baral
- *Is Retriever Merely an Approximator of Reader?* Sohee Yang,Minjoon Seo
- *TemporalWiki: A Lifelong Benchmark for Training and Evaluating Ever-Evolving Language Models* Joel Jang, Seonghyeon ye, Changho Lee, Sohee Yang, Joongbo Shin, Janghoon Han, Gyeonghun Kim, Minjoon Seo
- *Unsupervised Cross-Task Generalization via Retrieval Augmentation* Bill Yuchen Lin, Kangmin Tan, Chris Scott Miller, Beiwen Tian, Xiang Ren

- *Controllable Semantic Parsing via Retrieval Augmentation* Panupong Pasupat, Yuan Zhang, Kelvin Guu

- *StreamingQA: A Benchmark for Adaptation to New Knowledge over Timein Question Answering Models* Adam Liska, Tomas Kocisky, Elena Gribovskaya, Tayfun Terzi, Eren Sezener, Devang Agrawal, Cyprien de Masson d'Autume, Tim Scholtes, Manzil Zaheer, Susannah Young, Ellen Gilsenan-McMahon, Sophia Austin, Phil Blunsom, Angeliki Lazaridou

- *On the Effect of Pretraining Corpora on In-context Few-shot Learning by a Large-scale Language Model* Seongjin Shin, Sang-Woo Lee, Hwijeen Ahn, Sungdong Kim, HyoungSeok Kim, Boseop Kim, Kyunghyun Cho, Gichang Lee, Woomyoung Park, Jung-Woo Ha, Nako Sung

- *Exploring Dual Encoder Architectures for Question Answering* Zhe Dong, Jianmo Ni, Daniel M. Bikel, Enrique Alfonseca, Yuan Wang, Chen Qu, Imed Zitouni

Organizing Committee

Program Chairs

Rajarshi Das, University of Massachusetts Amherst
Patrick Lewis, University College London and Facebook AI Research
Sewon Min, University of Washington
June Thai, University of Massachusetts Amherst
Manzil Zaheer, Google DeepMind

Program Committee

Program Committee Members

Akari Asai, Paul G. Allen School of Computer Science and Engineering, University of Washington
Arthur Mensch, DeepMind
Ameya Godbole, University of Southern California
Ashwin Paranjape, Stanford University
Ahsaas Bajaj, University of Massachusetts, Amherst
Binh Vu, University of Southern California
Jean Maillard, Facebook AI
Jonathan Herzig, Tel Aviv University
Kevin Lin, University of California Berkeley
Kai Sun, Meta
Mor Geva, Allen Institute for Artificial Intelligence
Ni Lao, mosaix.ai
Peng Qi, JD AI Research
Devendra Singh Sachan, Mila - Quebec AI Institute
Shehzaad Zuzar Dhuliawala, Swiss Federal Institute of Technology
Shayne Longpre, Massachusetts Institute of Technology
Sohee Yang, Korea Advanced Institute of Science and Technology
Tong Wang, Microsoft
Urvashi Khandelwal, Google
Wenhan Xiong, Facebook
Yichen Jiang, Department of Computer Science, University of North Carolina, Chapel Hill
Yizhong Wang, Department of Computer Science, University of Washington
Yuxiang Wu, University College London

Invited Speakers

Danqi Chen, Princeton University
Hannaneh Hajishirzi, University of Washington and Allen Institute for AI
Andrew McCallum, University of Massachusetts, Amherst
Anna Potapenko, Google Deepmind
Jason Weston, Facebook AI Research

Table of Contents

Program

Friday, May 27, 2022

09:20 - 09:30	*Opening Remarks*
09:30 - 10:10	*Invited Talk 1: Anna Potapenko*
10:10 - 10:20	*Archival Track Contributed Talk: Efficient Machine Translation Domain Adaptation: Pedro Henrique Martins, Zita Marinho, Andre Martins*
10:20 - 10:30	*Non-Archival Track Contributed Talks 1: Internet-augmented language models through few-shot prompting for open-domain question answering: Angeliki Lazaridou, Elena Gribovskaya, Wojciech Stokowiec, Nikolai Grigorev*
10:30 - 10:40	*Non-Archival Track Contributed Talks 2: Towards Unsupervised Dense Information Retrieval with Contrastive Learning: Gautier Izacard, Mathilde Caron, Lucas Hosseini, Sebastian Riedel, Piotr Bojanowski, Armand Joulin, Edouard Grave*
10:40 - 10:50	*Non-Archival Track Contributed Talks 3: Towards Continual Knowledge Learning of Language Models: Joel Jang, Seonghyeon Ye, Sohee Yang, Joongbo Shin, Janghoon Han, Gyeonghun Kim, Stanley Jungkyu Choi, Minjoon Seo*
10:50 - 11:00	*Coffee Break*
11:00 - 12:00	*Poster Session I*
12:00 - 13:30	*Lunch Break*
13:30 - 14:10	*Invited Talk 2: Danqi Chen*
14:10 - 14:50	*Invited Talk 3: Jason Weston*
14:50 - 15:00	*Coffee Break*
15:00 - 16:00	*Poster Session II*
16:00 - 16:40	*Invited Talk 4: Andrew McCallum*
16:40 - 17:20	*Invited Talk 5: Hannah Hajishirzi*
17:20 - 17:50	*Panel Discussion*
17:50 - 18:00	*Closing Remarks*

Improving Discriminative Learning for Zero-Shot Relation Extraction

Van-Hien Tran[1]*, Hiroki Ouchi[1], Taro Watanabe[1], Yuji Matsumoto[2]
[1]Nara Institute of Science and Technology, Japan
{tran.van_hien.ts1,hiroki.ouchi,taro}@is.naist.jp
[2]RIKEN Center for Advanced Intelligence Project (AIP), Japan
yuji.matsumoto@riken.jp

Abstract

Zero-shot relation extraction (ZSRE) aims to predict target relations that cannot be observed during training. While most previous studies have focused on fully supervised relation extraction and achieved considerably high performance, less effort has been made towards ZSRE. This study proposes a new model incorporating discriminative embedding learning for both sentences and semantic relations. In addition, a self-adaptive comparator network is used to judge whether the relationship between a sentence and a relation is consistent. Experimental results on two benchmark datasets showed that the proposed method significantly outperforms the state-of-the-art methods.

1 Introduction

Relation extraction is a fundamental task in Natural Language Processing (NLP) that predicts the semantic relation between two entities in a given sentence. It has attracted considerable research effort as it plays a vital role in many NLP applications such as Information Extraction (Tran et al., 2021a,b) and Question Answering (Xu et al., 2016).

Most recent studies (Tran et al., 2019; Tian et al., 2021) treated this task in a fully supervised manner and achieved excellent performance. However, the supervised models cannot extract relations that are not predefined or observed during training, while many new relations always exist in real-world scenarios. Thus, it is worth enabling models to predict *new relations* that have never been seen before. Such a task is considered as zero-shot learning (Xian et al., 2019), where a key to achieving high performance is how to generalize a model to unseen classes by using a limited number of seen classes.

However, there are only a few existing studies on zero-shot relation extraction (ZSRE). Levy et al. (2017) tackled this task by using reading comprehension models with predefined question templates. Obamuyide and Vlachos (2018) simply reduced ZSRE to a text entailment task, utilizing existing textual entailment models. Recently, Chen and Li (2021) presented ZS-BERT, which projects sentences and relations into a shared space and uses the nearest neighbor search to predict unseen relations.

The previous studies overlooked the importance of learning discriminative embeddings. In essence, the discriminative learning helps models to better distinguish relations, especially on similar relations. Our study focuses on this aspect and demonstrates its significance for improving ZSRE. Specifically, we propose a new model that incorporates discriminative embedding learning (Han et al., 2021) for both sentences and semantic relations, which is inspired by contrastive learning (Chen et al., 2020) commonly used in computer vision. In addition, instead of using distance metrics to predict unseen relations as done by Chen and Li (2021), we use a self-adaptive comparator network to judge whether the relationship between a sentence and a relation is consistent. This verification process helps the model to learn more discriminative embeddings. Experimental results on two datasets showed that our method significantly outperforms the existing methods for ZSRE.

2 Related Work

To date, ZSRE has been under-investigated so far. Levy et al. (2017) formulated ZSRE as a question-answering task. They first manually created 10 question templates for each relation type and then trained a reading comprehension model. Because it requires the effort of hand-crafted labeling, this method can be unfeasible and impractical to define templates of new-coming unseen relations. Obamuyide and Vlachos (2018) converted ZSRE to a textual entailment task, in which the input sentence containing two entities is considered as the premise P, whereas the relation description containing the same entity pair is regarded as the hypothesis H.

* Corresponding author.

Proceedings of the 1st Workshop on Semiparametric Methods in NLP: Decoupling Logic from Knowledge, pages 1 - 6
May 27, 2022 ©2022 Association for Computational Linguistics

They then used existing textual entailment models (Rocktäschel et al., 2016; Chen et al., 2017) as their base models, although these models may not be entirely relevant for ZSRE. The closest to our work is research by Chen and Li (2021). First, they proposed the ZS-BERT model, which learns two functions to project sentences and relation descriptions into a shared embedding space. Then, they used the nearest neighbor search to predict unseen predictions; however, it is prone to suffer the hubness problem (Radovanovic et al., 2010). Unlike the previous studies, our work emphasizes the necessity of discriminative embedding learning that may play a vital role in solving the ZSRE.

3 Proposed Model

3.1 Task Definition

Let $\mathcal{Y}_S$ and $\mathcal{Y}_U$ denote the sets of *seen* and *unseen* relation labels, respectively. They are disjoint, *i.e.*, $\mathcal{Y}_S \cap \mathcal{Y}_U = \emptyset$. Given a training set with n_S samples, the ith sample consists of the input sentence X_i, the entities e_{i1} and e_{i2}, and the description D_i of the corresponding *seen* relation label $y_s^i \in \mathcal{Y}_S$, hereby denoted as $\left\{S_i = \left(X_i, e_{i1}, e_{i2}, D_i, y_s^i\right)\right\}_{i=1}^{n_S}$. Using the training set, we train a relation model $\mathcal{M}$, *i.e.*, $\mathcal{M}\left(S_i\right) \rightarrow y_s^i \in \mathcal{Y}_S$. In the test stage, given a testing sentence S' consisting of two entities and the descriptions of all *unseen* relation labels in $\mathcal{Y}_U$, $\mathcal{M}$ predicts the *unseen* relation $y_u^j \in \mathcal{Y}_U$ for S'.

3.2 Framework

Sentence Encoder. From the input sentence, we add four entity marker tokens ([E1], [/E1], [E2], and [/E2]) to annotate two entities, e_{i1} and e_{i2}. Then, we tokenize and input them through a pre-trained BERT encoder (Devlin et al., 2019). Finally, we obtain the vector representing the relation between the two entities by concatenating the two vectors of the start tokens ([E1] and [E2]).

Relation Encoder. Most relations are well defined, and their descriptions are available from open resources such as Wikidata (Chen and Li, 2021). For each relation, e.g., "*founded by*", we input its description to the pre-trained Sentence-BERT encoder (Reimers and Gurevych, 2019) and obtain the representation vector by using the mean pooling operation on the outputs.

Overview of the Model. On the basis of the two modules above, we present our full model in Figure 1. Given a training mini-batch of N sentences, we feed them into the **Sentence Encoder** and a subsequent nonlinear projector to obtain N final sentence embeddings. Simultaneously, we acquire K different relations from the N sentences. The K corresponding descriptions of the K relations are then fed into the **Relation Encoder** and a subsequent nonlinear projector to acquire the final relation embeddings. To obtain more discriminative embeddings, we introduce the learning constraints described in detail later. Finally, we concatenate pairs from the two spaces and use a network $\boldsymbol{F}$ to judge whether the relationship between a sentence and a relation is consistent.

3.3 Model Training

To boost the learning of discriminative embeddings for sentences and relations, we consider three main goals in training: (1) discriminative sentence embeddings, (2) discriminative relation embeddings, and (3) an effective comparator network $\boldsymbol{F}$.

Discriminative Sentence Embeddings. In Figure 1, given a mini-batch of N sentences, we obtain N corresponding sentence embeddings: $[\mathbf{s}_1, \mathbf{s}_2, \ldots, \mathbf{s}_N]$. To learn the discriminative features, we first use a softmax multi-class relation classifier to predict the seen relation for each sentence:

$$\mathcal{L}_{\text{Softmax}} = -\frac{1}{N}\sum_{i}^{N} y_s^i \log(\hat{y_s}^i), \tag{1}$$

where $y_s^i \in \mathcal{Y}_S$ is the ground-truth seen relation label of the ith sentence and $\hat{y_s}^i$ is the predicted probability of y_s^i. However, such a softmax loss only encourages the separability of the inter-class features. Meanwhile, discriminative power characterizes features in both the separable inter-class differences and the compact intra-class variations (Wen et al., 2016). Thus, we use another loss to ensure the intra-class compactness. First, the similarity distance between two sentences is given by

$$d\left(\mathbf{s}_i, \mathbf{s}_j\right) = 1/(1 + \exp(\frac{\mathbf{s}_i}{\|\mathbf{s}_i\|} \cdot \frac{\mathbf{s}_j}{\|\mathbf{s}_j\|})). \tag{2}$$

Clearly, this value should be small for any sentence pair of the same relation (*positive* pair) and large for a *negative* pair. We then apply such distance constraints on all T unordered sentence pairs, where

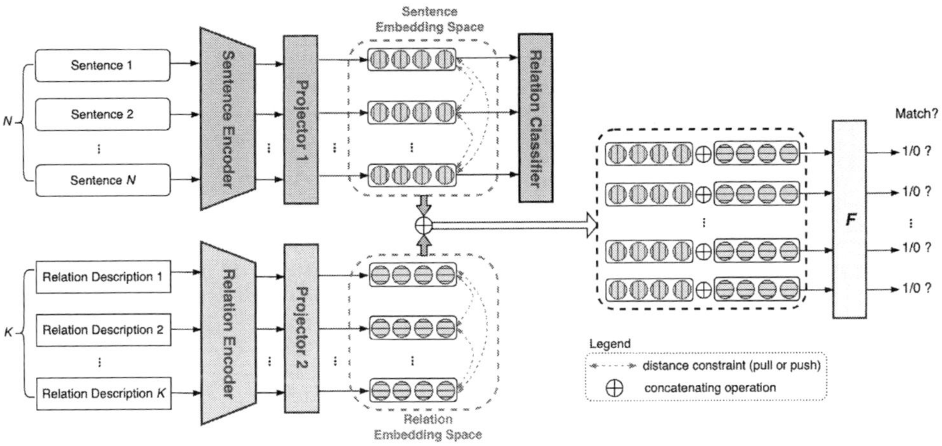

Figure 1: Overview of our proposed model with an input training mini-batch of size N.

$T = N(N-1)/2$, and formulate the loss as

$$\mathcal{L}_{\text{S2S}} = -\frac{1}{T}\sum_{i=1}^{N-1}\sum_{j=i+1}^{N}\Big(\mathbb{I}_{ij}\log d(\mathbf{s}_i,\mathbf{s}_j) + (1-\mathbb{I}_{ij})\log(1-d(\mathbf{s}_i,\mathbf{s}_j))\Big), \tag{3}$$

where $\mathbb{I}_{ij} = 1$ if the pair $(\mathbf{s}_i, \mathbf{s}_j)$ is *positive* or 0 otherwise. $\mathcal{L}_{\text{S2S}}$ not only ensures the intra-relation compactness but also encourages the inter-relation separability further. Finally, the final loss of learning discriminative sentence embeddings in the sentence embedding space is defined as follows:

$$\mathcal{L}_{sent} = \mathcal{L}_{Softmax} + \gamma \cdot \mathcal{L}_{\text{S2S}}, \tag{4}$$

where γ is a hyperparameter. With this joint supervision, it is expected that not only the inter-class sentence embedding differences are enlarged, but also the intra-class sentence embedding variations are reduced. Thus, the discriminative power of the learned sentence embeddings will be enhanced.

Discriminative Relation Embeddings. In Figure 1, we obtain K corresponding relation embeddings: $[\mathbf{r}_1, \mathbf{r}_2, \ldots, \mathbf{r}_K]$ for K different relations in the relation embedding space. From the K relations, we have a total of Q pairs ($Q = K(K-1)/2$), where each pair includes two different unordered relations. Thus, we maximize distance for each of these pairs and define the loss of learning discriminative relation embeddings by

$$\mathcal{L}_{rel} = -\frac{1}{Q}\sum_{i=1}^{K-1}\sum_{j=i+1}^{K}\log(1-d(\mathbf{r}_i,\mathbf{r}_j)), \tag{5}$$

where $d(\mathbf{r}_i, \mathbf{r}_j)$ is the similarity distance between two relations using Equation 2.

Comparator Network. After obtaining the discriminative embeddings of sentences and relations, we use a comparator network $\boldsymbol{F}$ to judge how well a sentence is consistent with a specific relation. This validation information will guide our model to learn more discriminative embeddings. In Figure 1, we concatenate sentences and relations as pairs and feed them into $\boldsymbol{F}$. To enhance the training efficiency, we control the rate of positive and negative pairs. Specifically, we keep all positive pairs but randomly keep only a part of negative pairs (e.g., positive:negative *rate* is 1:3). The $\boldsymbol{F}$ is a two-layer nonlinear neural network that outputs a scalar similarity score in the range of (0,1]. Finally, the loss of training $\boldsymbol{F}$ is defined as

$$\mathcal{L}_F = -\frac{\sum_{i=1}^{\mathcal{N}_{pos}}\log v_i + \sum_{j=1}^{\mathcal{N}_{neg}}\log(1-v_j)}{\mathcal{N}_{pos}+\mathcal{N}_{neg}}, \tag{6}$$

where v_i and v_j are the similarity scores of the ith positive pair and j^{th} negative pair, respectively; $\mathcal{N}_{pos}$ and $\mathcal{N}_{neg}$ are the number of positive pairs and negative pairs for training.

Total Loss. Based on the three aforementioned losses, the full loss function for training our model is as follows:

$$\mathcal{L} = \mathcal{L}_F + \alpha\mathcal{L}_{sent} + \beta\mathcal{L}_{rel}, \tag{7}$$

where α and β are hyperparameters that control the importance of $\mathcal{L}_{sent}$ and $\mathcal{L}_{rel}$, respectively.

3.4 Zero-Shot Relation Prediction

In the testing stage, we conduct zero-shot relation prediction by comparing the similarity score of a given sentence with all the unseen semantic relation representations. We classify the sentence $\mathbf{s}_i$ to the unseen relation that has the largest similarity score among relations, which can be formulated as

$$P_{zsre}(\mathbf{s}_i) = \max_j \{v_{ij}\}_{j=1}^{|\mathcal{Y}_{\mathcal{U}}|}. \quad (8)$$

4 Experiments

4.1 Dataset

Following the previous work (Chen and Li, 2021), we evaluate our model on two benchmark datasets: **Wiki-ZSL** and **FewRel** (Han et al., 2018). FewRel is a human-annotated balanced dataset consisting of 80 relation types, each of which has 700 instances. Wiki-ZSL is a subset of Wiki-KB dataset (Sorokin and Gurevych, 2017), which filters out both the "none" relation and relations that appear fewer than 300 times. The statistics of Wiki-KB, Wiki-ZSL, and FewRel are shown in Table 1. Note that descriptions of the relations in the above datasets are available and accessible from the open source Wikidata[1].

	#instances	#relations	avg. len.
Wiki-KB	1,518,444	354	23.82
Wiki-ZSL	94,383	113	24.85
FewRel	56,000	80	24.95

Table 1: The statistics of the datasets.

4.2 Experimental Settings

Following Chen and Li (2021), we randomly selected m relations as unseen ones ($m = |\mathcal{Y}_{\mathcal{U}}|$) for the testing set and split the entire dataset into the training and testing datasets accordingly. This guarantees that the m relations in the testing dataset do not appear in the training dataset. We used macro precision (*P*), macro recall (*R*), and macro F1-score (*F1*) as the evaluation metrics.

We implemented the neural networks using the PyTorch library[2]. The $tanh$ function is used with each nonlinear projector in our model. The comparator network $\boldsymbol{F}$ is a two-layer nonlinear neural network in which the hidden layer is equipped with the $tanh$ function, and the output layer size is outfitted with the $sigmoid$ function. The dropout technique was applied at a rate of 0.3 on the hidden layer and embeddings of sentences and relations in the two embedding spaces. We used Adam (Kingma and Ba, 2015) as the optimizer, in which the initial learning rate was $5e-6$; the batch size was 16 on FewRel and 32 on Wiki-ZSL; and $\alpha = 0.7$, $\beta = 0.3$, and $\gamma = 0.5$.

[1] https://www.wikidata.org/wiki/Wikidata:Main_Page

[2] PyTorch is an open-source software library for machine intelligence: https://pytorch.org/

	Wiki-ZSL			FewRel		
$m=5$	*P*	*R*	*F1*	*P*	*R*	*F1*
ESIM*	48.58	47.74	48.16	56.27	58.44	57.33
CIM*	49.63	48.81	49.22	58.05	61.92	59.92
ZS-BERT*	71.54	72.39	71.96	76.96	78.86	77.90
ZS-BERT†	74.32	71.72	72.97	80.96	78.00	79.44
Ours	**87.48**	**77.50**	**82.19**	**87.11**	**86.29**	**86.69**
$m=10$	*P*	*R*	*F1*	*P*	*R*	*F1*
ESIM*	44.12	45.46	44.78	42.89	44.17	43.52
CIM*	46.54	47.90	45.57	47.39	49.11	48.23
ZS-BERT*	60.51	60.98	60.74	56.92	57.59	57.25
ZS-BERT†	64.53	58.30	61.23	60.13	55.63	57.80
Ours	**71.59**	**64.69**	**67.94**	**64.41**	**62.61**	**63.50**
$m=15$	*P*	*R*	*F1*	*P*	*R*	*F1*
ESIM*	27.31	29.62	28.42	29.15	31.59	30.32
CIM*	29.17	30.58	29.86	31.83	33.06	32.43
ZS-BERT*	34.12	34.38	34.25	35.54	38.19	36.82
ZS-BERT†	35.42	33.47	34.42	39.09	36.70	37.84
Ours	**38.37**	**36.05**	**37.17**	**43.96**	**39.11**	**41.36**

Table 2: Results with different m values in percentage. * indicates the results reported by Chen and Li (2021); † marks the results we reproduced using the official source code of Chen and Li (2021).

4.3 Results and Analysis

Main Result. The experimental results obtained by varying m unseen relations are shown in Table 2. It can be observed that our model steadily outperforms the competing methods on the test datasets when considering different values of m. In addition, the improvement in our model is smaller when m is larger. An increase in m leads to a rise in the possible choices for prediction, thereby making it more difficult to predict the correct unseen relation.

Obamuyide and Vlachos (2018) simply used two basic text entailment models (ESIM and CIM) that may not be entirely relevant for ZSRE. Besides, they ignored the importance of discriminative feature learning for sentences and relations. Chen and Li (2021) also overlooked the necessity of learning discriminative embeddings. In addition, the nearest neighbor search method in ZS-BERT is prone to cause the hubness problem (Radovanovic et al., 2010). Thus, our model was designed to overcome the existing limitations. Compared with ZS-BERT, our model significantly improved its performance when $m = 5$, by 9.22 and 7.25 $F1$-score on Wiki-

$m = 5$	*F1*	
	Wiki-ZSL	FewRel
Ours	**82.19**	**86.69**
Ours ($\alpha = 0$)	74.42	81.05
Ours ($\beta = 0$)	78.92	84.27
Ours ($\gamma = 0$)	77.13	82.95

Table 3: Ablation study.

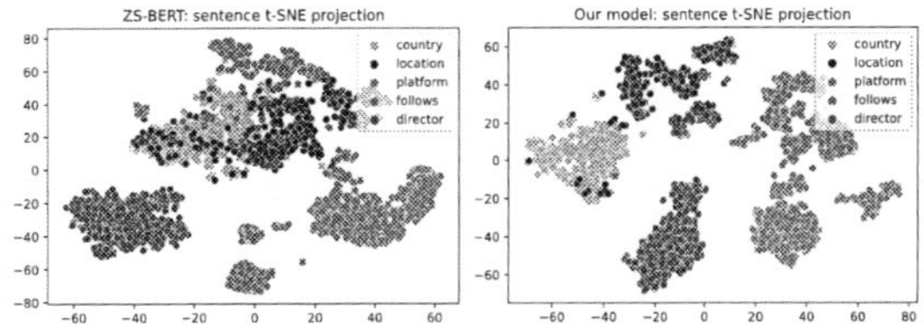

Figure 2: Visualization of the sentence embeddings by ZS-BERT and our model when $m = 5$ on the FewRel.

ZSL and FewRel, respectively.

Impact of Discriminative Learning. To gain more insight into the improvement in our model, we analyzed the importance of learning discriminative features in both the sentence and relation spaces. In Table 3, we consider three special cases of Equation 7: (1) $\alpha = 0$ means no $\mathcal{L}_{sent}$; (2) $\beta = 0$ means no $\mathcal{L}_{rel}$; and (3) $\gamma = 0$ means no $\mathcal{L}_{S2S}$, which is a part of $\mathcal{L}_{sent}$. Clearly, all three losses are important for training our model to obtain the best performance. In particular, $\mathcal{L}_{sent}$ for learning discriminative sentence features is more important than $\mathcal{L}_{rel}$ for learning discriminative relation embeddings, as the performance decreases significantly after removing it. In addition, $\mathcal{L}_{S2S}$ plays a vital role in $\mathcal{L}_{sent}$ since it mainly ensures the intra-relation compactness property of discriminative sentence embeddings.

Feature Space Visualization. We visualized the testing sentence embeddings produced by ZS-BERT and our model in a case of $m = 5$ on the FewRel[3] dataset using t-SNE (Maaten and Hinton, 2008). Figure 2 shows that the embeddings generated by our model express not only a larger inter-relation separability but also a better intra-relation compactness, compared with the embeddings by ZS-BERT. Besides, we focus on two relations: "country" and "location". According to their descriptions (country[4] and location[5]), we can see that they are somewhat similar but different in some details. Specifically, an ordered entity pair (***e1***, ***e2***) in a sentence expresses the relation "country" if and only if ***e2*** must be a country and ***e2*** has sovereignty over ***e1***. Meanwhile, if the entity pair (***e1***, ***e2***) does not hold the relation "country", it may appear the relation "location" when ***e2*** is a place that ***e1*** happens or exists. Thus, the two similar relations make it difficult for ZS-BERT to distinguish them. Meanwhile, our model can discriminate between them. These observations again prove the necessity of learning discriminative features for ZSRE.

5 Conclusion

In this work, we present a new model to solve the ZSRE task. Our model aims to enhance the discriminative embedding learning for both sentences and relations. It boosts inter-relation separability and intra-relation compactness of sentence embeddings and maximizes distances between different relation embeddings. In addition, a comparator network is used to validate the consistency between a sentence and a relation. Experimental results on two benchmark datasets demonstrated the superiority of the proposed model for ZSRE.

References

Chih-Yao Chen and Cheng-Te Li. 2021. ZS-BERT: Towards zero-shot relation extraction with attribute representation learning. In *Proceedings of the 2021 Conference of the North American Chapter of the Association for Computational Linguistics: Human Language Technologies*, pages 3470–3479, Online. Association for Computational Linguistics.

Qian Chen, Xiaodan Zhu, Zhen-Hua Ling, Si Wei, Hui Jiang, and Diana Inkpen. 2017. Enhanced LSTM for natural language inference. In *Proceedings of the 55th Annual Meeting of the Association for Computational Linguistics (Volume 1: Long Papers)*, pages 1657–1668, Vancouver, Canada. Association for Computational Linguistics.

Ting Chen, Simon Kornblith, Mohammad Norouzi, and Geoffrey Hinton. 2020. A simple framework for contrastive learning of visual representations. In *Proceedings of the 37th International Conference on Machine Learning*, volume 119 of *Proceedings of Machine Learning Research*, pages 1597–1607. PMLR.

Jacob Devlin, Ming-Wei Chang, Kenton Lee, and Kristina Toutanova. 2019. BERT: Pre-training of

[3]The FewRel dataset is annotated by crowdworkers, thereby ensuring high quality.

[4]`https://www.wikidata.org/wiki/Property:P17`

[5]`https://www.wikidata.org/wiki/Property:P27`

deep bidirectional transformers for language understanding. In *Proceedings of the 2019 Conference of the North American Chapter of the Association for Computational Linguistics: Human Language Technologies, Volume 1 (Long and Short Papers)*, pages 4171–4186, Minneapolis, Minnesota. Association for Computational Linguistics.

Jiale Han, Bo Cheng, and Guoshun Nan. 2021. Learning discriminative and unbiased representations for few-shot relation extraction. In *Proceedings of the 30th ACM International Conference on Information amp; Knowledge Management*, CIKM '21, page 638–648, New York, NY, USA. Association for Computing Machinery.

Xu Han, Hao Zhu, Pengfei Yu, Ziyun Wang, Yuan Yao, Zhiyuan Liu, and Maosong Sun. 2018. FewRel: A large-scale supervised few-shot relation classification dataset with state-of-the-art evaluation. In *Proceedings of the 2018 Conference on Empirical Methods in Natural Language Processing*, pages 4803–4809, Brussels, Belgium. Association for Computational Linguistics.

Diederik P. Kingma and Jimmy Ba. 2015. Adam: A method for stochastic optimization. In *3rd International Conference on Learning Representations, ICLR 2015, San Diego, CA, USA, May 7-9, 2015, Conference Track Proceedings*.

Omer Levy, Minjoon Seo, Eunsol Choi, and Luke Zettlemoyer. 2017. Zero-shot relation extraction via reading comprehension. In *Proceedings of the 21st Conference on Computational Natural Language Learning (CoNLL 2017)*, pages 333–342, Vancouver, Canada. Association for Computational Linguistics.

Laurens van der Maaten and Geoffrey Hinton. 2008. Visualizing data using t-sne. *Journal of Machine Learning Research*, 9(86):2579–2605.

Abiola Obamuyide and Andreas Vlachos. 2018. Zero-shot relation classification as textual entailment. In *Proceedings of the First Workshop on Fact Extraction and VERification (FEVER)*, pages 72–78, Brussels, Belgium. Association for Computational Linguistics.

Milos Radovanovic, Alexandros Nanopoulos, and Mirjana Ivanovic. 2010. Hubs in space: Popular nearest neighbors in high-dimensional data. *Journal of Machine Learning Research*, 11:2487–2531.

Nils Reimers and Iryna Gurevych. 2019. Sentence-BERT: Sentence embeddings using Siamese BERT-networks. In *Proceedings of the 2019 Conference on Empirical Methods in Natural Language Processing and the 9th International Joint Conference on Natural Language Processing (EMNLP-IJCNLP)*, pages 3982–3992, Hong Kong, China. Association for Computational Linguistics.

Tim Rocktäschel, Edward Grefenstette, Karl Moritz Hermann, Tomás Kociský, and Phil Blunsom. 2016. Reasoning about entailment with neural attention. In *4th International Conference on Learning Representations, ICLR 2016, San Juan, Puerto Rico, May 2-4, 2016, Conference Track Proceedings*.

Daniil Sorokin and Iryna Gurevych. 2017. Context-aware representations for knowledge base relation extraction. In *Proceedings of the 2017 Conference on Empirical Methods in Natural Language Processing*, pages 1784–1789, Copenhagen, Denmark. Association for Computational Linguistics.

Yuanhe Tian, Guimin Chen, Yan Song, and Xiang Wan. 2021. Dependency-driven relation extraction with attentive graph convolutional networks. In *Proceedings of the 59th Annual Meeting of the Association for Computational Linguistics and the 11th International Joint Conference on Natural Language Processing (Volume 1: Long Papers)*, pages 4458–4471, Online. Association for Computational Linguistics.

Van-Hien Tran, Van-Thuy Phi, Akihiko Kato, Hiroyuki Shindo, Taro Watanabe, and Yuji Matsumoto. 2021a. Improved decomposition strategy for joint entity and relation extraction. *Journal of Natural Language Processing*, 28(4):965–994.

Van-Hien Tran, Van-Thuy Phi, Hiroyuki Shindo, and Yuji Matsumoto. 2019. Relation classification using segment-level attention-based CNN and dependency-based RNN. In *Proceedings of the 2019 Conference of the North American Chapter of the Association for Computational Linguistics: Human Language Technologies, Volume 1 (Long and Short Papers)*, pages 2793–2798, Minneapolis, Minnesota. Association for Computational Linguistics.

Vu Tran, Van-Hien Tran, Phuong Nguyen, Chau Nguyen, Ken Satoh, Yuji Matsumoto, and Minh Nguyen. 2021b. CovRelex: A COVID-19 retrieval system with relation extraction. In *Proceedings of the 16th Conference of the European Chapter of the Association for Computational Linguistics: System Demonstrations*, pages 24–31, Online. Association for Computational Linguistics.

Yandong Wen, Kaipeng Zhang, Zhifeng Li, and Yu Qiao. 2016. A discriminative feature learning approach for deep face recognition. In *Computer Vision – ECCV 2016*, pages 499–515. Springer International Publishing.

Yongqin Xian, Christoph H. Lampert, Bernt Schiele, and Zeynep Akata. 2019. Zero-shot learning—a comprehensive evaluation of the good, the bad and the ugly. *IEEE Transactions on Pattern Analysis and Machine Intelligence*, 41(9):2251–2265.

Kun Xu, Siva Reddy, Yansong Feng, Songfang Huang, and Dongyan Zhao. 2016. Question answering on Freebase via relation extraction and textual evidence. In *Proceedings of the 54th Annual Meeting of the Association for Computational Linguistics (Volume 1: Long Papers)*, pages 2326–2336, Berlin, Germany. Association for Computational Linguistics.

Choose Your QA Model Wisely: A Systematic Study of Generative and Extractive Readers for Question Answering

Man Luo [1,2,*] **Kazuma Hashimoto**[2] **Semih Yavuz**[2]
Zhiwei Liu[2] **Chitta Baral**[1] **Yingbo Zhou**[2]
[1] Arizona State University [2] Salesforce Research
[1] {mluo26, chitta}@asu.edu
[2]{k.hashimoto, syavuz, zhiweiliu, yingbo.zhou}salesforce.com

Abstract

While both extractive and generative readers have been successfully applied to the Question Answering (QA) task, little attention has been paid toward the systematic comparison of them. Characterizing the strengths and weaknesses of the two readers is crucial not only for making a more informed reader selection in practice but also for developing a deeper understanding to foster further research on improving readers in a principled manner. Motivated by this goal, we make the first attempt to systematically study the comparison of extractive and generative readers for question answering. To be aligned with the state-of-the-art, we explore nine transformer-based large pre-trained language models (PrLMs) as backbone architectures. Furthermore, we organize our findings under two main categories: (1) keeping the architecture invariant, and (2) varying the underlying PrLMs. Among several interesting findings, it is important to highlight that (1) the generative readers perform better in long context QA, (2) the extractive readers perform better in short context while also showing better out-of-domain generalization, and (3) the encoder of encoder-decoder PrLMs (e.g., T5) turns out to be a strong extractive reader and outperforms the standard choice of encoder-only PrLMs (e.g., RoBERTa). We also study the effect of multi-task learning on the two types of readers varying the underlying PrLMs and perform qualitative and quantitative diagnosis to provide further insights into future directions in modeling better readers.

1 Introduction

Question Answering (QA) is an important task to evaluate the reading comprehension capacity of an intelligent system and can be directly applied to real applications such as search engines (Kwiatkowski et al., 2019) and dialogue systems (Reddy et al., 2019; Choi et al., 2018). This paper studies extractive QA which is a specific type of QA; i.e., answering the question using a span from the context (Rajpurkar et al., 2016; Fisch et al., 2019). Extractive readers (Seo et al., 2017; Devlin et al., 2019) are widely used to tackle such a task, where the goal is to classify start and end positions of the answer in the context. Generative readers (Raffel et al., 2020; Lewis et al., 2020c; Izacard and Grave, 2021) have also shown remarkable performance, where the goal is to generate answers by autoregressively predicting tokens.

Both the state-of-the-art extractive and generative readers are based on large pretrained language models (PrLMs) and show good performance on different datasets. However, a systematic comparison between them has been largely unexplored. Such a comparison reveals the strengths and weaknesses of each reader, which in turn can provide more principled guidance on which reader and PrLM should be applied in which cases, and also open up future research opportunities grounded on identified concrete challenges to improve reader models. However fair comparisons between these have been difficult to perform mainly because 1) the PrLMs for extractive and generative are different, i.e., extractive readers are usually built on top of encoder-only PrLM while generative ones are based on encoder-decoder PrLMs, and 2) the size of generative and extractive readers are not the same, which can greatly affect the performance. We design two main set of controlled experiments to address such challenges in comparing extractive and generative readers in a principled manner.

In the first set of experiments, we compare extractive and generative readers using the same PrLMs. Specifically, T5 (Raffel et al., 2020) generative reader is compared with T5 extractive reader and similarly for BART (Lewis et al., 2020a). This allows a fair comparison of different answer prediction approaches without being affected by different architecture or prior knowledge of PrLMs. More-

*Work done during internship at Salesforce Research.

Proceedings of the 1st Workshop on Semiparametric Methods in NLP: Decoupling Logic from Knowledge, pages 7 - 22
May 27, 2022 ©2022 Association for Computational Linguistics

over, we challenge the conventional formulation of extractive readers, which are often built upon encoder-only PrLMs, by leveraging the encoder of encoder-decoder PrLMs as a variable alternative. More concretely, we use the encoders of T5 and BART models to explore their capacity as an extractive reader to better understand the effect of different pre-training strategies on the final QA performance.

While the aforementioned comparison strategy adopts the same PrLMs, it remains unclear how generative readers compare with the conventional extractive readers that are built upon encoder-only PrLMs. Thus, in the second experiment, we compare different architecture PrLMs, including T5, BART, ELECTRA (Clark et al., 2020) and RoBERTa (Liu et al., 2019), to draw more generalizable and grounded conclusions. All models in this suite of experiments have similar sizes, thus reducing the impact of model size on performance.

With these two experiments, we present a systematic comparison of extractive and generative readers using nine readers on the MRQA task (Fisch et al., 2019), a collection of multiple extractive QA datasets. This evaluation results in five insightful findings:

1. The first experiment reveals that the choice of PrLM affects the performance. Specifically, for T5, the generative reader is better than the extractive one, but for BART, extractive readers are better than the generative ones.
2. The second experiment shows that on average, extractive readers performs better than the generative ones, with the extractive reader built on the encoder of T5 performing the best among the different types of PrLMs.
3. Extractive readers perform better in short context and have better generalization on out-of-domain datasets and rare answers, but the generative readers perform better in the long context.
4. The encoder of encoder-decoder PrLMs are also good extractive readers. Extractive readers built on top of the encoder of BART or T5 are better than encoder-only PrLMs, like RoBERTa.
5. While the inference length is usually chosen to be the same as in the training time, we find that longer inference length has a positive effect for all PrLMs. Using longer lengths for long contexts leads to greater gains than short contexts.

Our work presents an in-depth study of extractive and generative readers for QA task, an important NLP task toward building intelligent systems. Our findings shed light on key considerations behind reader selection and would be helpful for formulating future research on advancing reader models.

2 Related Work

Pretrained Language Models Here, we mainly discuss two types of pre-trained models based on transformers architecture (Vaswani et al., 2017), autoencoder and encoder-decoder models, which are widely used for QA tasks. Autoencoder only relies on the encoder part in the original transformer, and in the pretraining time, the input is a corrupted sentence, for example, a sentence with mask tokens, such as BERT (Devlin et al., 2019) and RoBERTa (Liu et al., 2019) and ELECTRA (Clark et al., 2020). Both RoBERTa and ELECTRA has the same architecture as BERT but perform better than BERT on many tasks. RoBERTa mainly benefits from larger training corpus consisting of news, books, stories, and web text. ELECTRA adapts GAN-style training (Mirza and Osindero, 2014) and aims to detect if a token is replaced or is from the original text. Large ELECTRA is trained on similar data as RoBERTa. BART (Lewis et al., 2020b) and T5 (Raffel et al., 2020) belong to encoder-decoder architecture. BART is pretrained on the same data as RoBERTa, while T5 is pretrained on Colossal Clean Common Crawl Corpus as well as the multiple downstream tasks.

Question Answering Systems We focus on QA systems that are built upon PrLMs. Extractive QA readers assume that answers can be found in the context and aim to predict the corresponding start and end tokens from the context (Fisch et al., 2019; Li et al., 2019; Clark et al., 2020; Karpukhin et al., 2020). Differently, generative QA readers are not restricted to the input context, where they can freely generate answers token by token using the entire vocabulary in an autoregressive manner (Raffel et al., 2020). Generative readers are more often used in open domain (Lewis et al., 2020c; Izacard and Grave, 2021; Xiong et al., 2021) and unified settings (Khashabi et al., 2020; Tafjord and Clark, 2021). Fajcik et al. (2021) combines extractive and generative readers by adding a classification module to decide which reader predicts answers. Cheng et al. (2021) proposes a unified system of extractive and generative readers, but different from (Fajcik et al., 2021), the output is computed by both extractive and generative readers.

3 Model

We mainly study the QA models based on PrLMs with extractive and generative approaches.

3.1 Extractive Reader

In extractive reader, an encoder firstly receives the concatenation of a question $\mathbf{q} : \{q_1, \ldots, q_t\}$ and a context $\mathbf{c} : \{c_1, \ldots, c_m\}$, where q_i and c_j are tokens in question and context, respectively. Then, it produces $\mathbf{h} : [h_1|\cdots|h_m] \in \mathbb{R}^{d \times m}$, where h_j corresponds to the d-dimensional contextual representation of context token c_j. We then stack two linear layers on top of the contextual representations to independently predict the probability of each context token being start and end positions of the correct answer. More formally, given a tuple $(\mathbf{q}, \mathbf{c}, \mathbf{a})$, where $\mathbf{a}$ is an answer, the training objective is to minimize the following loss function

$$\mathcal{L}_{\text{Ext}} = -\log(\mathbf{P}_{\mathbf{start,s}}) - \log(\mathbf{P}_{\mathbf{end,e}}) \quad (1)$$

where $\mathbf{P}_{\mathbf{start}}, \mathbf{P}_{\mathbf{end}} \in \mathbb{R}^m$ are defined by

$$\mathbf{P}_{\mathbf{start}} = \text{softmax}(\mathbf{w}_{\mathbf{start}}\mathbf{h}) \quad (2)$$
$$\mathbf{P}_{\mathbf{end}} = \text{softmax}(\mathbf{w}_{\mathbf{end}}\mathbf{h}) \quad (3)$$

where $\mathbf{w}_{\mathbf{start}}$ and $\mathbf{w}_{\mathbf{end}}$ denote for the linear layers to predict start and end tokens, $\mathbf{P}_{\mathbf{start,s}}$ and $\mathbf{P}_{\mathbf{end,e}}$ denote the probability of the ground truth start and end tokens of answer $\mathbf{a}$, respectively. In testing time, the answer span is decoded by $\text{argmax}_{i,j}\{\mathbf{P}_{\mathbf{start,i}} \times \mathbf{P}_{\mathbf{end,j}}\}$.

In this work, we have two variants of extractive readers. One is encoder-only models to get the contextual representation of each token. We call such kind of reader as **E-Extractive reader**. Apart from taking the conventional PrLMs such as RoBERTa and ELECTRA, we also apply the encoder part in T5 and BART to be E-Extractive reader. The other one is using the encoder-decoder models where the decoder is to obtained the contextual representation of each token in the context in an autoregressive way (see §3.2). We use both BART and T5 PrLMs and term this kind of reader as **ED-Extractive reader**.

3.2 Generative Reader

We consider a generative reader consisting of an encoder and a decoder where the decoder is used to generate answers in an autoregressive way. Specially, the encoder takes a question $\mathbf{q}$ and a context $\mathbf{c}$ as input and outputs contextual representation $\mathbf{h}$. Then, the decoder takes the previously generated answer tokens as input and performs attention over $\mathbf{h}$ and then generates the next token. Formally, given a tuple $(\mathbf{q}, \mathbf{c}, \mathbf{a})$, the training objective is to minimize the following loss function

$$\mathcal{L}_{\text{Gen}} = \sum_{i=1}^{K} \log \mathbf{P}(a_i \mid \mathbf{h}, a_{:i}) \quad (4)$$

where K is the number of tokens in answer $\mathbf{a}$, a_i is the ith token in $\mathbf{a}$, and a_0 corresponds to a special beginning of sequence (`BOS`) token. In the inference time, we use the greedy search method to autoregressively generate the answer.

Dataset	Training size	Avg. tokens in Q	Avg. tokens in C
In-domain datasets			
SQuAD	86,588	11.53	144.15
NewsQA	74,160	7.60	581.61
TriviaQA	61,688	15.81	782.59
SearchQA	117,384	17.46	744.44
HotpotQA	72,928	18.89	237.67
NQ	104,071	9.18	158.80
Out-of-domain datasets			
DROP	-	11.18	215.16
RACE	-	11.82	347.90
BioASQ	-	11.53	252.83
TextbookQA	-	11.07	663.36
RE	-	9.26	30.02
DuoRC	-	8.63	732.92

Table 1: Statistics of In-domain (IID) and out-of-domain (OOD) datasets of MRQA benchmark.

4 Experiments

4.1 Dataset

We conduct experiments on MRQA benchmark which provides six in-domain (IID) datasets, and six out-of-domain (OOD) datasets for generalization evaluation. MRQA covers different domains (e.g. News and biomedical) and different types of questions, (e.g. single hop and multi-hop). Table 1 shows the statistic of each IID and OOD dataset. Some datasets have long context and others are short context. More details about MRQA are presented in Appendix A.

4.2 Learning Strategy

Single Task Learning: we use each IID datasets to train extractive and generative readers. **Multi-Task Learning:** we consider training with all (six) IID datasets as multi-task learning for two reasons. As (Su et al., 2019) showed that different IID datasets share a low similarity, therefore, they may require different reasoning skills. In addition, Table 1 shows that different datasets have different question and context lengths, which may lead to different difficulties between datasets.

4.3 Experimental Setup

We use Huggingface (Wolf et al., 2020) and Pytorch (Paszke et al., 2019) implementation for training each model. All models are trained using maximum input length of 512 and other details is provided in Appendix B[1]. In Table 2, we summarize the size of each evaluated model and the size of PrLMs are chosen based on a comparable way and the best computation power. For example, we choose T5 base model for generative reader since the large T5 is too larger (737M).

Input Format: Given a question **Q** and a context **C**, the input to extractive readers is {**Q** [SEP] **C**} and the input to generative readers is {*question:* **Q** [SEP] *context:* **C**}. We also considered other input formats, which are reported in Appendix C.

Answer Length of Generative Reader: We set the maximum generated answer length as 16 for generative reader. Using longer generation lengths (32 and 64) do not yield noticeable improvement as reported in Appendix D.

5 Results and Analysis

We first present the study of using different inference length for each model since it guides us to choose the best performance of each model. Then, we compare the generative and extractive readers using the same PrLMs and the different PrLMs. Last, we present a detail analysis to diagnose the difference among extractive and generative reader. F1 is used to measure performance. Note that since we test each model on 12 datasets, the observation and conclusion we draw are mostly based on the average across all datasets.

5.1 The Effect of Context Length

While all models are trained with 512 maximum length, the inference length can be longer than this. We experiment with three lengths, 512, 1024, and the full length of input question and context. Due to the tokenization and pretraining maximum length of each PrLM, ELECTRA only allows 512 maximum inference length, RoBERTa and BART allows 1024, and T5 allows the full length of input.

We present the average performance of each model on both IID and OOD in Table 3[2], from which three trends are observed. (1) When using 512 inference length, ELECTRA is the best model in single-task learning on IID datasets and multi-task in both IID and OOD datasets. (2) Increasing the inference length actually improves all models' performance. (3) The length affects the T5 models more significantly than others, for example, in single-task learning, the largest improvement of length 1024 for T5 model on IID and OOD datasets are 2.77% and 5.49%, while for other models, the largest improvement of length 1024 compared to 512 are 1.32% and 1.65%. The performance of using 512 and 1024 are given in Appendix E, and we present the performance of each dataset using the best input length in the following sections.

5.2 Comparison within Same PrLMs

We compare different readers when using the same PrLMs. Two PrLMs, T5 and BART, are considered, where T5-base model is applied to each T5 reader, and BART-large model is applied to each BART reader. We have three comparison as there are two types of extractive and one type of generative readers (§3). We present the average performance in each comparison and the detail performance on each datasets are given in Appendix F.

ED-Extractive and E-Extractive Since the E-Extractive reader is only use the encoder part of the PrML without the decoder, the size of E-Extractive reader is less than the ED-Extractive. But even under this disadvantage, surprisingly, we find that the encoder part actually perform well on QA tasks. In Figure 1 , the red and green bars compare the ED-Extractive and E-Extractive reader. For BART model, the E-Extractive reader outperforms ED-Extractive reader on average on IID and OOD datasets in single task learning as well as multi-task learning. This indicates that the decoder in BART is not crucial for the extractive reader. On the other hand, for T5, the ED-Extractive reader outperforms E-Extractive reader on average on both IID and OOD datasets. This suggests that the decoder in T5 still plays a role to yield better performance. But the performances are similar even that the E-Extractive reader has less parameters.

[1]While we fix the training hyperparameters for all the models for the sake of experimental efficiency, the performance of our setting is close to the original results.

[2]Note that in single-task learning, the performance on OOD are extracted from the best performance of each single-task model on every dataset and this applies to all other tables in this paper.

	T5 E-Ext	T5 E-Ext	T5 ED-Ext	T5 ED-Gen	Bart E-Ext	Bart ED-Ext	Bart ED-Gen	ELECTRA	RoBERTa
Size	base	large	base	base	large	large	large	large	large
# Params (M)	110	335	223	223	204	406	406	334	354

Table 2: Size and parameters of readers. ED: encoder-decoder, Ext for extractive, Gen for generative approach.

Model	In-domain Avg.			Out-of-domain Avg.		
	512	1024	Full	512	1024	Full
Single Task Learning						
T5 E-Ext (B)	74.42	75.80	**77.93**	55.89	58.06	**58.65**
T5 E-Ext (L)	76.46	78.67	**80.85**	60.74	63.67	**64.49**
T5 ED-Ext (B)	74.75	77.06	**79.11**	57.11	59.19	**59.99**
T5 ED-Gen (B)	77.91	80.68	**81.02**	56.26	61.75	**61.82**
BART E-Ext (L)	77.78	**79.10**	-	59.67	**61.32**	-
BART ED-Ext (L)	77.10	**77.34**	-	**59.29**	59.21	-
BART ED-Gen (L)	69.89	**70.24**	-	49.65	**53.51**	-
RoBERTa (L)	77.59	**77.89**	-	60.32	**60.47**	-
ELECTRA (L)	78.71	-	-	60.19	-	-
Multi-Task Learning						
T5 E-Ext (B)	75.74	76.65	**78.99**	58.94	61.55	**61.98**
T5 E-Ext (L)	77.10	79.30	**81.55**	63.04	66.10	**66.78**
T5 ED-Ext (B)	75.92	77.38	**79.93**	59.23	61.86	**62.64**
T5 ED-Gen (B)	78.06	80.89	**81.16**	57.82	63.56	**63.68**
BART E-Ext (L)	77.75	**79.13**	-	63.27	**64.06**	-
BART ED-Ext (L)	77.26	**77.55**	-	62.14	**62.68**	-
BART ED-Gen (L)	78.11	**78.55**	-	57.41	**60.54**	-
RoBERTa (L)	77.86	**78.02**	-	**63.70**	63.58	-
ELECTRA (L)	78.52	-	-	63.83	-	-

Table 3: Result of each model using three inference length. **Bold** number means the highest value of each model with three inference length for IID and OOD datasets. L: large PrLMs, B: base PrLMs

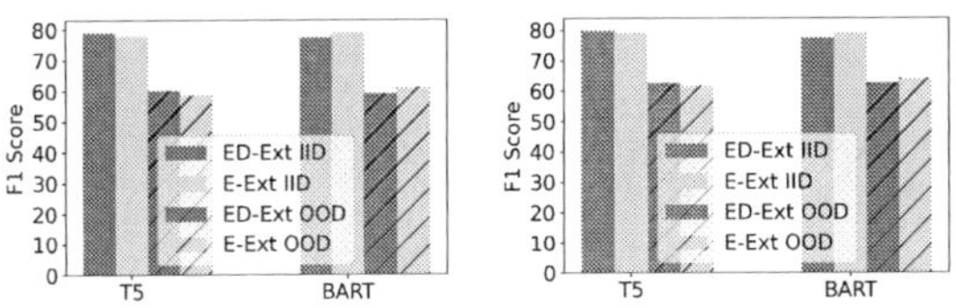

Figure 1: Left for single-task and right for multi-tasks settings. For T5, ED-Ext performs better than E-Ext reader; for BART, E-Ext is better than ED-Ext reader even though the former has less parameters.

ED-Extractive and ED-Generative Reader Here, the model size of extractive reader and generative reader are almost the same (see Table 2) and also the pre-owned knowledge of two readers are the same since both readers use the encoder and decoder parts. In Figure 2, the red and blue bars compare the ED-Extractive and ED-Generative reader. For T5, generative models performs better than the extractive one on four cases, IID and OOD datasets and single- and multi-tasks learning. For BART PrLM, in single-task learning, the extractive model is much better than the generative model. This probably explains why in most of the previous work, when BART is applied to extractive QA tasks, it is used as extractive reader even though it belongs to encoder-decoder model family[3]. The story for multi-task learning is different, and we find that the BART generative reader benefits significantly from multi-task learning and even outperforms the BART ED-extractive reader on IID datasets. It indicates that the decoder in BART requires larger and more diversified datasets to learn the QA task.

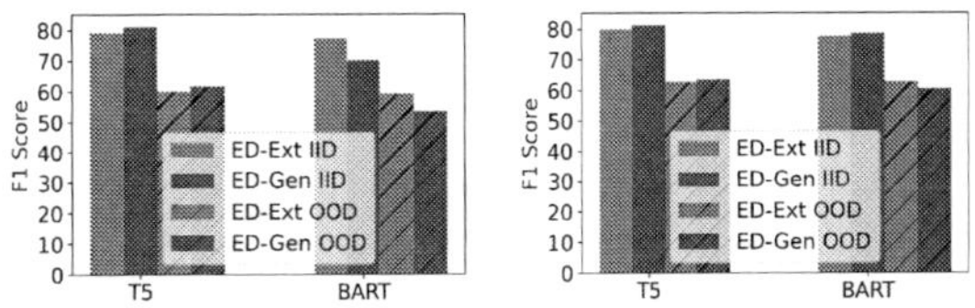

Figure 2: Left for single-task and right for multi-tasks settings. For T5, ED-Gen performs better than ED-Ext; For BART, ED-Ext is better than ED-Gen in single task learning, but worse in multi-task learning on IID.

E-Extractive and Generative Reader In this comparison, the extractive reader has less advantage than the generative ones since the decoder has been removed in E-Extractive reader. In Figure 3, the green and blue bars compare the E-Extractive and ED-Generative reader. For T5 model, the generative reader are better than the extractive ones in both single- and multi-tasks and IID and OOD datasets. But again, this disadvantages of extractive readers might come from the smaller model size as we discussed in previous comparison. For BART model, E-Extractive reader outperforms generative reader significantly on both IID and OOD datasets and the advantage of E-Extractive reader are much more significantly in single-task learning scenario. To summarize,

1. The encoder part itself in both T5 and BART can perform well as an extractive reader.

[3]The original BART paper takes BART as an extractive and also the implementation of using BART for QA in Huggingface library do the same.

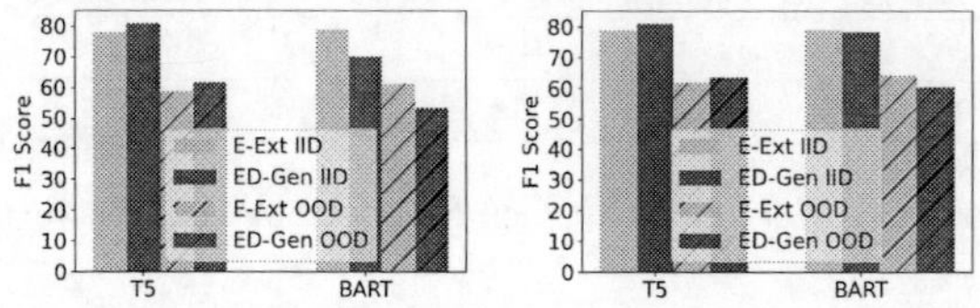

Figure 3: Left for single-task and right for multi-tasks settings. For T5, ED-Gen is better than E-Ext reader; for BART, E-Ext is better than ED-Gen reader even though the former has less parameters.

2. The comparison among three types of reader using BART and T5 suggests that although both PrLMs are of encoder-decoder architecture, three types of readers behave quite differently. This might caused by different pre-training objectives and knowledge.
3. For BART model, the E-Extractive reader outperforms ED-Extractive reader and generative reader regardless of less parameters, thus should be used as an extractive reader.
4. The BART generative reader requires large and diversified datasets to learn the QA task and thus benefits significantly from multi-task learning.
5. For T5, the performance of generative reader consistently outperforms two types of extractive reader. The deficiency of T5-Extractive reader might be caused by less parameters.

5.3 Comparison within Different PrLMs

The previous section compares the generative and extractive readers using the same PrLMs and both PrLMs are encoder-decoder models. On one hand, such comparison reduces the impacts of PrLMs architecture and pre-owned knowledge. On the other hand, it raises two concerns. First, whether extractive readers using an encoder-decoder PrLMs are good for representatives of extractive readers? After all, encoder-only PrLMs are more standard choice for extractive readers in most previous work. Second, whether the smaller size of the extractive reader cause its deficiency compared to the generative one, particularly that the T5 E-Extractive reader is half size of the T5 generative reader in previous comparison.

To clear out the first concern, here, we present the comparison cross different PrLMs including standard encoder-only models for extractive readers. To address the second concern, we carefully select the model size so that each model is of relative comparable size.

The Selection of Each Model's size We use the encoder in T5 large model for the T5 E-Extractive reader so that it is of similar size as RoBERTa and ELECTRA extractive readers ($\sim$330M)[4]. When using BART PrLMs for extractive reader, we only use BART E-Extractive reader but not ED-Extractive reader because the former performs better even though it has less parameters (204M) than the later one has larger size. T5 generative reader is also smaller (223M), but this is better than using T5 large generative reader to compare with others, which is way too larger than other readers (737M). For BART generative reader, it is larger than other readers (406M). One potential issue for the above-mentioned setting is that even though we choose the best comparison setting, still each model size are different, and thus if a model perform inferior than others, it might due to the smaller model size. However, the following conclusion we draw does not effect by this issue.

Are Encoder-decoder PrLMs Good for Extractive Readers? Based on Table 4, we find that encoder-decoder PrLMs outperform encoder-only PrLMs as extractive readers on average. Both T5 and BART E-Extractive readers perform better than RoBERTa and ELECTRA on IID and OOD datasets under single- as well as multi-task learning regardless of less parameters of T5 and BART. This observation is exciting since instead of using standard encoder-only PrLMs for extractive reader, encoder-decoder PrLMs are actually better choice.

Which reader generalize better on OOD? The extractive reader generalize better on OOD datasets. In both single- and multi-task learning, T5 E-Extractive reader shows the best performance, especially beating the BART generative reader even though the latter one has more parameters. BART E-Extractive reader also generalize well on OOD, and it also beats the BART generative reader even though the former has less parameters than the later.

Which PrLM is the best? Based on Table 4, we see that T5 is the best among four PrLMs in both single- and multi-tasks learning scenario on IID as well as OOD datasets. We observe two advantages of T5 over other PrLMs. First, T5 is much better than ELECTRA and RoBERTa on NewsQA data. In both single- and multi- task learning, RoBERTa

[4]Note that the T5 PrLM is already trained on SQuAD, while others do not. However, based on the results on SQuAD, T5 does not have advantage over other models on this dataset.

Model	In-domain Datasets							Out-of-domain Datasets							
	SQuAD	NewsQA	TQA	SQA	HQA	NQ	Avg.	DROP	RACE	BioASQ	TbQA	RE	DuoRC	Avg.
Single Task Learning														
T5 ED-Gen	90.75	71.65	**79.61**	**86.21**	79.89	78.04	**81.02**	48.08	48.89	67.36	<u>60.30</u>	84.94	<u>61.35</u>	<u>61.82</u>
BART ED-Gen	78.75	66.20	67.81	78.89	73.22	56.58	70.24	44.22	43.70	55.59	45.11	76.83	55.63	53.51
T5 E-Ext	92.47	**72.63**	76.09	<u>83.24</u>	80.67	**80.00**	<u>80.85</u>	53.14	**52.06**	**71.26**	**61.92**	85.78	**62.80**	**64.49**
BART E-Ext	92.19	<u>72.20</u>	73.12	77.19	80.61	<u>79.29</u>	79.10	51.57	48.82	<u>68.83</u>	51.29	86.04	<u>61.35</u>	61.32
ELECTRA	**93.39**	60.23	<u>76.31</u>	82.54	<u>80.99</u>	78.78	78.71	<u>55.43</u>	<u>49.80</u>	66.96	47.80	<u>86.23</u>	54.90	60.19
RoBERTa	<u>92.64</u>	59.95	72.97	81.62	**81.21**	78.95	77.89	**55.88**	47.72	64.47	52.31	**86.69**	55.75	60.47
Multi-Task Learning														
T5 ED-Gen	91.41$_{+0.66}$	71.29$_{-0.36}$	**80.01**$_{+0.40}$	**86.46**$_{+0.25}$	79.70$_{-0.19}$	78.09$_{+0.05}$	<u>81.16</u>$_{+0.14}$	51.20$_{+3.12}$	49.66$_{+0.77}$	68.72$_{+1.36}$	<u>62.90</u>$_{+2.60}$	85.84$_{+0.90}$	<u>63.76</u>$_{+2.41}$	63.68$_{+1.86}$
BART ED-Gen	88.63$_{+9.88}$	68.91$_{+2.71}$	74.91$_{+7.10}$	82.52$_{+3.63}$	80.53$_{+7.31}$	75.78$_{+19.20}$	78.55$_{+8.31}$	55.20$_{+10.98}$	50.04$_{+6.34}$	63.78$_{+8.19}$	54.81$_{+9.70}$	80.94$_{+4.11}$	58.47$_{+2.84}$	60.54$_{+7.03}$
T5 E-Ext	92.84$_{+0.37}$	**73.51**$_{+0.88}$	<u>77.37</u>$_{+1.28}$	82.89$_{-0.35}$	81.92$_{+1.25}$	**80.74**$_{+0.74}$	**81.55**$_{+0.70}$	59.10$_{+5.96}$	**54.01**$_{+1.95}$	<u>71.13</u>$_{-0.13}$	**64.90**$_{+2.98}$	86.53$_{+0.75}$	**65.01**$_{+2.21}$	**66.78**$_{+2.29}$
BART E-Ext	92.46$_{+0.27}$	<u>72.11</u>$_{-0.09}$	72.24$_{-0.88}$	76.53$_{-0.66}$	82.04$_{+1.43}$	79.40$_{+0.11}$	79.13$_{+0.03}$	58.22$_{+6.65}$	50.40$_{+1.58}$	70.72$_{+1.89}$	56.29$_{+5.00}$	<u>86.79</u>$_{+0.75}$	61.95$_{+0.60}$	<u>64.06</u>$_{+2.74}$
ELECTRA	<u>93.27</u>$_{-0.12}$	60.59$_{+0.36}$	72.96$_{-3.35}$	82.03$_{-0.51}$	**83.10**$_{+2.11}$	79.16$_{+0.38}$	78.52$_{-0.19}$	<u>62.56</u>$_{+7.13}$	50.29$_{+0.49}$	**71.50**$_{+4.54}$	54.60$_{+6.80}$	**87.14**$_{+0.91}$	56.88$_{+1.98}$	63.83$_{+3.64}$
RoBERTa	**93.41**$_{+0.77}$	59.56$_{-0.39}$	72.23$_{-0.74}$	80.98$_{-0.64}$	82.37$_{+1.16}$	<u>79.55</u>$_{+0.60}$	78.02$_{+0.13}$	**64.47**$_{+8.59}$	<u>51.81</u>$_{+4.09}$	69.15$_{+4.68}$	53.68$_{+1.37}$	86.31$_{-0.38}$	56.06$_{+0.31}$	63.58$_{+3.11}$

Table 4: Comparison of readers based on the different PrLMs by F1 Score. Inference length of T5 is full length of context, 512 for ELECTRA, and 1024 for BART and RoBERTa. TQA: TriviaQA; SQA:SearchQA; HQA:HotpotQA; NQ: NaturalQuestions; TbQA:TextbookQA; RE:RelationExtraction. **Bold** numbers denote for the best result and <u>underline</u> numbers for the second best.

and ELECTRA achieve around 60% F1 score on NewsQA, while both T5 extractive and generative reader achieved higher than 70% F1 score, yielding more than 10% improvements. Second, T5 is better at long context dataset. In IID, TQA and SQA, T5 ED-Generative reader outperforms other readers at least 3.30% and 3.67% in single-task, 7.05% and 4.43% in multi-task learning. On OOD datasets, TbQA and DuoRC, T5 E-Extractive reader is better than others at least by 9.61% and 1.45% in single-task, 8.61% and 3.06% in multi-task. We would like to mention that this advantage of T5 is conditioned on using full inference length, when using short input length such as 512, this advantage does not exhibit as we shown in §5.1.

Which PrLM benefits more from Multi-task Learning? While multi-task learning is in general beneficial for all PrLMs, we find BART benefits the most from multi-task learning, especially for the generative reader. For example, on IID datasets. BART generative reader improves more than 8% on average while all other readers improves less than 1%. Similarly for OOD datasets, the improvement of multi-task learning on BART generative reader are more significant than other readers. To summarize,

1. Encoder-decoder PrLMs can be in fact used as extractive readers, they are even better than the conventional choice (encoder-only PrLMs) of extractive readers on average.
2. Extractive readers perform better than the generative readers on OOD datasets, especially for the ones based on the encoder-decoder PrLMs.
3. T5 is the best among four PrLMs since it performs better on the news domain and the long context. And the advantage of T5 is conditioned on using full inference length.
4. While in general multi-task learning turns out to be useful for all PrLMs, BART PrLM benefits the most.

5.4 In-Depth Diagnosis

We investigate the behavior of extractive and generative models in long and short context and predicting answers which include rare characters. Multi-task models in §5.3 are chosen for comparison.

5.4.1 Long and Short Context

As we discussed in previous section that generative readers have advantage over extractive counterparts. To further support this trend, we divide the testing sets into five subsets, where we count the total words in question and context, and choose five thresholds, 2/4/6/8/10 hundreds. It is worth to mention that since all extractive readers use the window-stride strategy (i.e. if the input length is longer than the maximum length, then the input is segmented into multiple inputs), so that the entire context is observable for extractive readers.

From Figure 4, we have two observations. First, on IID datasets, for questions and contexts with less than 600 words, the extractive ones always perform better than the generative ones (the dash lines are higher than the solid ones), but when the length are more than 600 words, the generative ones consistently outperform the extractive ones. This suggests that the extractive readers performs better in the short context while the generative readers perform better in long context. Second, on OOD datasets, T5 generative reader still presents advantage in the long context (more than 600 words), while BART

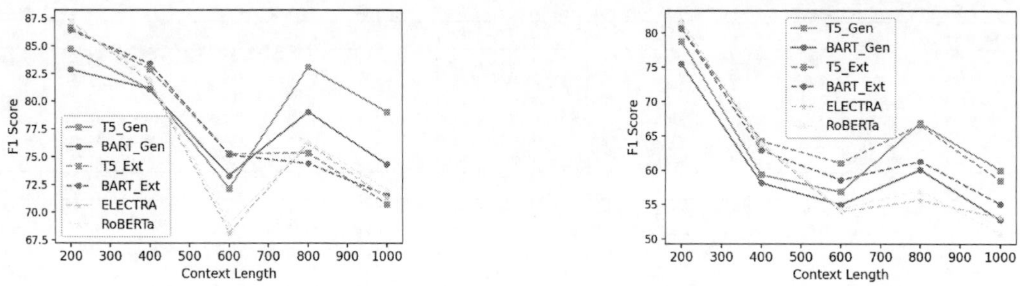

Figure 4: Comparison among generative and extractive readers on different length of the question and context. Left part for IID and right part for OOD datasets. Dash line for extractive and solid line for generative readers.

generative reader performs worse than the extractive one in both short and long context. But the gap between the BART generative and extractive readers is less on the long context compared to the short context. It might suggest that the extractive reader has better generalization capacity than the generative one thus the advantage of generative reader in long context is weakened.

5.4.2 Rare Characters in Answer

We find that some answers of testing sets include rare characters such as *ń* and *ł* (119 are found), thus we divide the testing sets into two subsets, one is the normal answer set where the answer does not have rare characters[5], the other one is with rare characters. The percentage of rare cases for IID and OOD datasets is 1.4% and 2%, respectively.

From Table 5, we have two observations. First, in normal case, the performance of extractive and generative readers are relatively comparable on both IID and OOD datasets, but in rare case, the extractive readers are better than the generative ones This suggests that the extractive reader has better generalization than the generative ones. Second, we see that the rare tokens has worse impact on T5 than BART generative readers in both in- and out-of-domain datasets. Further investigation finds that 94 out of 119 rare characters can not be represented by T5 tokenizer (i.e. T5 tokenizer uses '<unk>' special tokens to represent these characters), and tends to ignore these special characters in the generation time as the two examples shown in Table 6. Differently, BART tokenizer can represent all rare characters. Improving generative readers performance in predicting rare answers is an important future work. To summarize,

1. Extractive readers performs better than the generative reader on short context, but generative one performs better on long context.
2. Generative readers performs worse in predicting answers with rare characters, and T5 performs worse than BART.

Answer type	**Domain**	**Gen**		**Ext**			
		T5	BART	T5	BART	Ro	EL
Rare	IID	68.97	73.64	77.79	**78.54**	78.64	78.18
	OOD	59.25	79.84	**85.22**	84.95	80.73	86.94
Normal	IID	**82.71**	80.02	79.98	79.95	80.35	78.18
	OOD	68.28	64.19	**69.9**	66.91	67.75	68.12

Table 5: Compare extractive and generative readers in terms of rare and normal answers. Ro for RoBERTa and EL for ELECTRA.

Question	**Answer**	**Prediction**
Who was one of the most famous people born in Warsaw?	Maria Skłodowskacurie	Maria Skodowska-Curie
What museum preserves the memory of the crime?	Katyń Museum	Katy Museum

Table 6: Examples of questions with answers containing rare characters and the prediction of T5-Gen.

6 Conclusion and Future Work

We systematically compare the extractive and generative readers for QA tasks. Two sets of experiments are designed to control the effects of different PrLMs and the size of models. By conducting experiments on 12 QA datasets, our findings provide guidelines on how to choose extractive or generative readers given their strength and weakness.

While current work investigates the pros and cons of extractive and generative models systematically, there are some hyperparameters that might

[5]Rare characters are any characters which are not belongs to the printable characters in the string library of Python. The printable characters include lower and upper case alphabets, digits, punctuation, and white-space.

affect the model performance. For example, it is known that different prompts in the input effect generative model performance (Mishra et al., 2021b,a). Also, it is worth studying the OOD performance of models deeply. Gokhale et al. (2022) compares multiple ways to improve the OOD performance of an extractive model on QA task, and how these methods affect generative models have not been well-studied yet. Meanwhile, most of the work including this work evaluate OOD performance by averaging the performance across multiple dataset, but as mentioned in (Mishra et al., 2020), the evaluation should be more carefully designed. Also, Diagnosing the performance on each OOD dataset can provide more insights. For example, why models perform better on BioASQ dataset than most other datasets (see Table 4), while previous work have shown that it is hard to transfer general model to biomedical domain (Luo et al., 2022). Investigating the reason behind the observations and improving the generative and extractive models are interesting research questions for future.

References

Hao Cheng, Yelong Shen, Xiaodong Liu, Pengcheng He, Weizhu Chen, and Jianfeng Gao. 2021. UnitedQA: A hybrid approach for open domain question answering. In *Proceedings of the 59th Annual Meeting of the Association for Computational Linguistics and the 11th International Joint Conference on Natural Language Processing (Volume 1: Long Papers)*, pages 3080–3090, Online. Association for Computational Linguistics.

Eunsol Choi, He He, Mohit Iyyer, Mark Yatskar, Wentau Yih, Yejin Choi, Percy Liang, and Luke Zettlemoyer. 2018. QuAC: Question answering in context. In *Proceedings of the 2018 Conference on Empirical Methods in Natural Language Processing*, pages 2174–2184, Brussels, Belgium. Association for Computational Linguistics.

Kevin Clark, Minh-Thang Luong, Quoc V. Le, and Christopher D. Manning. 2020. Electra: Pretraining text encoders as discriminators rather than generators. *ArXiv*, abs/2003.10555.

Jacob Devlin, Ming-Wei Chang, Kenton Lee, and Kristina Toutanova. 2019. BERT: Pre-training of deep bidirectional transformers for language understanding. In *Proceedings of the 2019 Conference of the North American Chapter of the Association for Computational Linguistics: Human Language Technologies, Volume 1 (Long and Short Papers)*, pages 4171–4186, Minneapolis, Minnesota. Association for Computational Linguistics.

Martin Fajcik, Martin Docekal, Karel Ondrej, and P. Smrz. 2021. Pruning the index contents for memory efficient open-domain qa. *ArXiv*, abs/2102.10697.

Adam Fisch, Alon Talmor, Robin Jia, Minjoon Seo, Eunsol Choi, and Danqi Chen. 2019. MRQA 2019 shared task: Evaluating generalization in reading comprehension. In *Proceedings of the 2nd Workshop on Machine Reading for Question Answering*, pages 1–13, Hong Kong, China. Association for Computational Linguistics.

Tejas Gokhale, Swaroop Mishra, Man Luo, Bhavdeep Singh Sachdeva, and Chitta Baral. 2022. Generalized but not robust? comparing the effects of data modification methods on out-of-domain generalization and adversarial robustness. *arXiv preprint arXiv:2203.07653*.

Gautier Izacard and Edouard Grave. 2021. Leveraging passage retrieval with generative models for open domain question answering. In *Proceedings of the 16th Conference of the European Chapter of the Association for Computational Linguistics: Main Volume*, pages 874–880, Online. Association for Computational Linguistics.

Vladimir Karpukhin, Barlas Oguz, Sewon Min, Patrick Lewis, Ledell Wu, Sergey Edunov, Danqi Chen, and Wen-tau Yih. 2020. Dense passage retrieval for open-domain question answering. In *Proceedings of the 2020 Conference on Empirical Methods in Natural Language Processing (EMNLP)*, pages 6769–6781, Online. Association for Computational Linguistics.

Daniel Khashabi, Sewon Min, Tushar Khot, Ashish Sabharwal, Oyvind Tafjord, Peter Clark, and Hannaneh Hajishirzi. 2020. UNIFIEDQA: Crossing format boundaries with a single QA system. In *Findings of the Association for Computational Linguistics: EMNLP 2020*, pages 1896–1907, Online. Association for Computational Linguistics.

Tom Kwiatkowski, Jennimaria Palomaki, Olivia Redfield, Michael Collins, Ankur Parikh, Chris Alberti, Danielle Epstein, Illia Polosukhin, Jacob Devlin, Kenton Lee, Kristina Toutanova, Llion Jones, Matthew Kelcey, Ming-Wei Chang, Andrew M. Dai, Jakob Uszkoreit, Quoc Le, and Slav Petrov. 2019. Natural questions: A benchmark for question answering research. *Transactions of the Association for Computational Linguistics*, 7:452–466.

Mike Lewis, Yinhan Liu, Naman Goyal, Marjan Ghazvininejad, Abdelrahman Mohamed, Omer Levy, Veselin Stoyanov, and Luke Zettlemoyer. 2020a. Bart: Denoising sequence-to-sequence pretraining for natural language generation, translation, and comprehension. In *Proceedings of the 58th Annual Meeting of the Association for Computational Linguistics*, pages 7871–7880.

Mike Lewis, Yinhan Liu, Naman Goyal, Marjan Ghazvininejad, Abdelrahman Mohamed, Omer

Levy, Veselin Stoyanov, and Luke Zettlemoyer. 2020b. BART: Denoising sequence-to-sequence pre-training for natural language generation, translation, and comprehension. In *Proceedings of the 58th Annual Meeting of the Association for Computational Linguistics*, pages 7871–7880, Online. Association for Computational Linguistics.

Patrick Lewis, Ethan Perez, Aleksandara Piktus, Fabio Petroni, Vladimir Karpukhin, Naman Goyal, Heinrich Kuttler, M. Lewis, Wen tau Yih, Tim Rocktäschel, Sebastian Riedel, and Douwe Kiela. 2020c. Retrieval-augmented generation for knowledge-intensive nlp tasks. *ArXiv*, abs/2005.11401.

Hongyu Li, Xiyuan Zhang, Yibing Liu, Yiming Zhang, Quan Wang, Xiangyang Zhou, Jing Liu, Hua Wu, and Haifeng Wang. 2019. D-NET: A pre-training and fine-tuning framework for improving the generalization of machine reading comprehension. In *Proceedings of the 2nd Workshop on Machine Reading for Question Answering*, pages 212–219, Hong Kong, China. Association for Computational Linguistics.

Yinhan Liu, Myle Ott, Naman Goyal, Jingfei Du, Mandar Joshi, Danqi Chen, Omer Levy, M. Lewis, Luke Zettlemoyer, and Veselin Stoyanov. 2019. Roberta: A robustly optimized bert pretraining approach. *ArXiv*, abs/1907.11692.

Man Luo, Arindam Mitra, Tejas Gokhale, and Chitta Baral. 2022. Improving biomedical information retrieval with neural retrievers. *arXiv preprint arXiv:2201.07745*.

Mehdi Mirza and Simon Osindero. 2014. Conditional generative adversarial nets. *ArXiv*, abs/1411.1784.

Swaroop Mishra, Anjana Arunkumar, Chris Bryan, and Chitta Baral. 2020. Our evaluation metric needs an update to encourage generalization. *arXiv preprint arXiv:2007.06898*.

Swaroop Mishra, Daniel Khashabi, Chitta Baral, Yejin Choi, and Hannaneh Hajishirzi. 2021a. Reframing instructional prompts to gptk's language. *arXiv preprint arXiv:2109.07830*.

Swaroop Mishra, Daniel Khashabi, Chitta Baral, and Hannaneh Hajishirzi. 2021b. Cross-task generalization via natural language crowdsourcing instructions. *arXiv preprint arXiv:2104.08773*.

Adam Paszke, Sam Gross, Francisco Massa, Adam Lerer, James Bradbury, Gregory Chanan, Trevor Killeen, Zeming Lin, Natalia Gimelshein, Luca Antiga, Alban Desmaison, Andreas Kopf, Edward Yang, Zachary DeVito, Martin Raison, Alykhan Tejani, Sasank Chilamkurthy, Benoit Steiner, Lu Fang, Junjie Bai, and Soumith Chintala. 2019. Pytorch: An imperative style, high-performance deep learning library. In H. Wallach, H. Larochelle, A. Beygelzimer, F. d'Alché-Buc, E. Fox, and R. Garnett, editors, *Advances in Neural Information Processing Systems 32*, pages 8024–8035. Curran Associates, Inc.

Colin Raffel, Noam M. Shazeer, Adam Roberts, Katherine Lee, Sharan Narang, Michael Matena, Yanqi Zhou, W. Li, and Peter J. Liu. 2020. Exploring the limits of transfer learning with a unified text-to-text transformer. *ArXiv*, abs/1910.10683.

Pranav Rajpurkar, Jian Zhang, Konstantin Lopyrev, and Percy Liang. 2016. SQuAD: 100,000+ questions for machine comprehension of text. In *Proceedings of the 2016 Conference on Empirical Methods in Natural Language Processing*, pages 2383–2392, Austin, Texas. Association for Computational Linguistics.

Siva Reddy, Danqi Chen, and Christopher D. Manning. 2019. CoQA: A conversational question answering challenge. *Transactions of the Association for Computational Linguistics*, 7:249–266.

Minjoon Seo, Aniruddha Kembhavi, Ali Farhadi, and Hannaneh Hajishirzi. 2017. Bidirectional attention flow for machine comprehension. *ArXiv*, abs/1611.01603.

Dan Su, Yan Xu, Genta Indra Winata, Peng Xu, Hyeondey Kim, Zihan Liu, and Pascale Fung. 2019. Generalizing question answering system with pre-trained language model fine-tuning. In *Proceedings of the 2nd Workshop on Machine Reading for Question Answering*, pages 203–211, Hong Kong, China. Association for Computational Linguistics.

Oyvind Tafjord and Peter Clark. 2021. General-purpose question-answering with macaw.

Ashish Vaswani, Noam M. Shazeer, Niki Parmar, Jakob Uszkoreit, Llion Jones, Aidan N. Gomez, Lukasz Kaiser, and Illia Polosukhin. 2017. Attention is all you need. *ArXiv*, abs/1706.03762.

Thomas Wolf, Lysandre Debut, Victor Sanh, Julien Chaumond, Clement Delangue, Anthony Moi, Pierric Cistac, Tim Rault, Remi Louf, Morgan Funtowicz, Joe Davison, Sam Shleifer, Patrick von Platen, Clara Ma, Yacine Jernite, Julien Plu, Canwen Xu, Teven Le Scao, Sylvain Gugger, Mariama Drame, Quentin Lhoest, and Alexander Rush. 2020. Transformers: State-of-the-art natural language processing. In *Proceedings of the 2020 Conference on Empirical Methods in Natural Language Processing: System Demonstrations*, pages 38–45, Online. Association for Computational Linguistics.

Wenhan Xiong, Xiang Lorraine Li, Srini Iyer, Jingfei Du, Patrick Lewis, William Yang Wang, Yashar Mehdad, Wen tau Yih, Sebastian Riedel, Douwe Kiela, and Barlas Ouguz. 2021. Answering complex open-domain questions with multi-hop dense retrieval. *ArXiv*, abs/2009.12756.

A More Details of MRQA Datasets

MRQA provides six datasets for training and six for out-of-domain evaluations. In Table 7, we present the source of each datasets, and we can see that the domains are diversified. Figure 5 and 6 show the histogram of the context length of IID and OOD dataset. The distribution shows that some datasets are mainly short, some are mainly long, and others are the combination of short and long. We use short annotation for some datasets, TQA: TriviaQA; SQA:SearchQA; HQA:HotpotQA; NQ: NaturalQuestions; TbQA:TextbookQA; RE:RelationExtraction.

Dataset	Source
SQuAD	Wikipedia
NewsQA	News article
TQA	Trivia and quiz-league websites
SQA	Jeopardy! TV show
HQA	Wikipedia
NQ	Wikipedia
DROP	Wikipedia
RACE	English reading comprehension exams for middle and high school
BioASQ	Science (PubMed) articles
TbQA	Lessons from middle school Life Science, Earth Science, and Physical Science textbooks
RE	Wikiread
DuoRC	wikipedia

Table 7: The source of each dataset

B Training Setup

We use Huggingface (Wolf et al., 2020) implementation and Pytorch (Paszke et al., 2019) to train each model. All model are trained on 4 GTX1080 GPUs in 4 epochs with a learning rate of 1e-4, batch size of 128, random seed 1234. While we fix these hyperparameters for all models, we get similar results as the original paper (i.e. the difference in terms of F1 are mostly within 2 percent.) In details, on SQuAD dataset, RoBERTa in (Liu et al., 2019) and in ours achieves 94.6 and 92.64 F1 scores, respectively; BART in (Lewis et al., 2020a) and in ours achieves 94.6 and 92.51 F1 scores, respectively; ELECTRA in (Clark et al., 2020) and in ours achieves 94.2 and 93.39 F1 scores, respectively; T5 in (Raffel et al., 2020) and in ours achieves 80.88 and 82.56 EM scores, respectively.

C Two Input Format

When fine-tuning generative reader on question answering task, some special words are added before the real input to denote the type of task. In an extractive reader, usually, there are no special words added. Here, we evaluate these two formats for T5 and BART generative reader. Particularly, given a question **Q** and a context **C**, format 1 is to add the "question:" and "context:" in front of the real question and context such that the input is {*question:* **Q** [SEP] *context:* **C**}; and format 2 is without these special words such that the input is {**Q** [SEP] **C**}. To keep the training process be efficient, we evaluate on two datasets SearchQA and HotpotQA, instead of all datasets. Table 8 shows that format 1 yields slightly better performance for T5 and much better performance for BART on SQA datasets, and thus we use this format for all generative reader.

Model	Format	SQA		HQA	
		EM	F1	EM	F1
T5	1	81.07	86.21	64.04	79.89
	2	80.65	85.76	63.23	79.42
BART	1	72.86	78.89	55.77	73.22
	2	49.28	58.00	55.72	73.20

Table 8: Comparison between different input format on two datasets. Format1 means input with "question:" and "context:" as format1, and format2 means without.

D Answer Length of Generative Reader

For the generative reader, we tried different maximum lengths of the generated answer: 16, 32, and 64. Table 9 shows that increasing the length of the target does not make improvement, this might be because the answer in the testing data is usually short and thus length of 16 is sufficient.

E Inference Length

We present the results of using 512 and 1024 length and full length in Table 10, 11, 12 separately. Note that due the tokenization approach adapted by each model, for Electra using 1024 or full length is same as using 512, for RoBERTa and BART, using full length is the same as length 1024. Furthermore, the detailed performance of each single task model is given in Table 14, using the best inference of each model, i.e. full length for T5, 1024 for RoBERTa and BART, and 512 for ELECTRA.

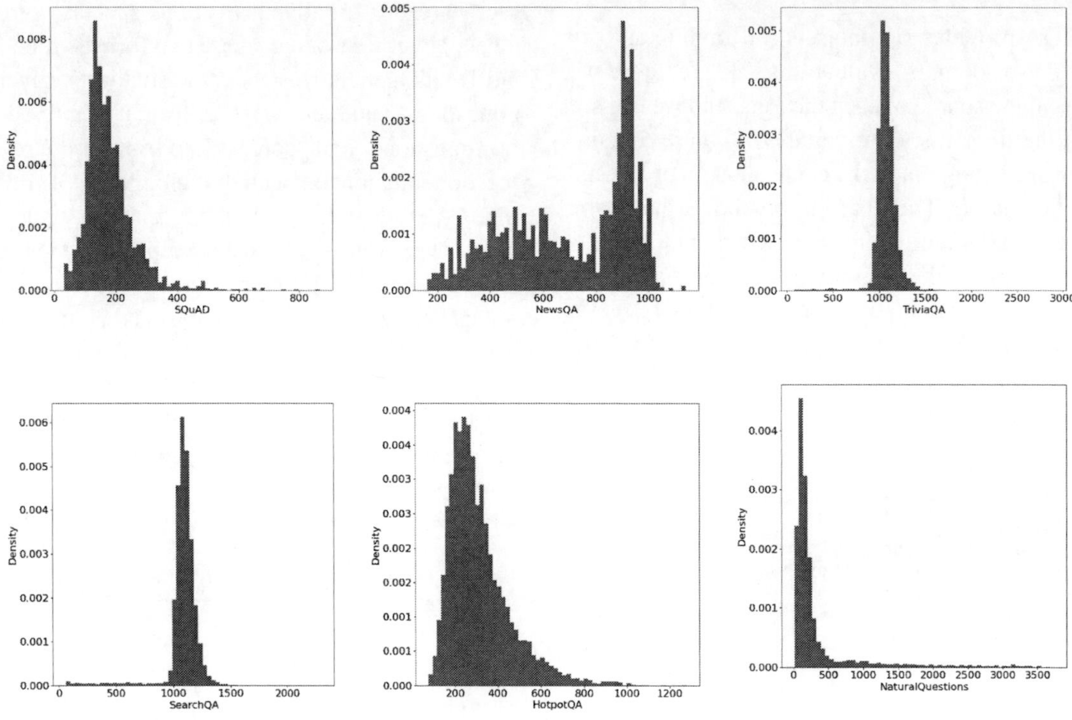

Figure 5: Context Length Histogram of In-domain dataset

F Detailed Comparison Results for Using Same PrLMs

Table 13 presents the F1 score of each readers when using the same PrLMs as we discussed in §5.2.

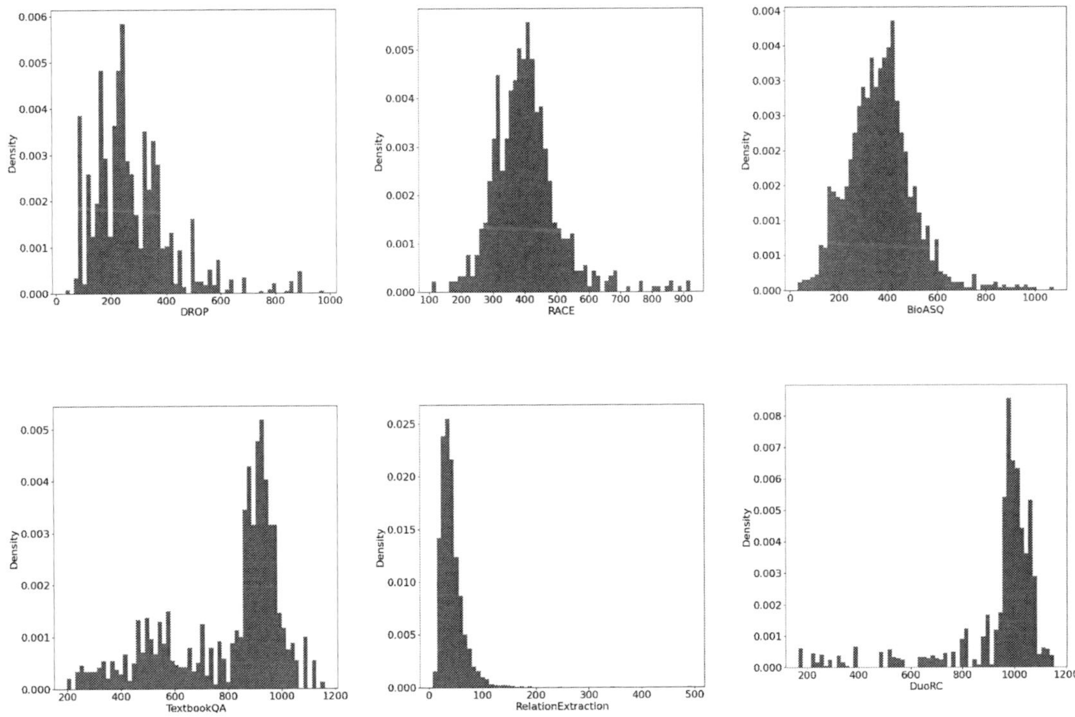

Figure 6: Context Length Histogram of out-domain dataset

Length	IID Datasets							OOD Datasets						
	SQuAD	NewsQA	TQA	SQA	HQA	NQ	Avg.	DROP	RACE	BioASQ	TbQA	RE	DuoRC	Avg.
16	91.41	71.29	80.01	86.46	79.7	78.09	81.16	51.2	49.66	68.72	62.9	85.84	63.76	63.68
32	91.41	71.29	80.01	86.46	79.7	78.09	81.16	51.2	49.66	68.72	62.9	85.84	63.76	63.68
64	91.41	71.29	80.01	86.46	79.7	78.09	81.16	51.2	49.66	68.72	62.9	85.84	63.76	63.68
16	88.63	68.91	74.91	82.52	80.53	75.78	78.55	55.2	50.04	63.78	54.81	80.94	58.47	60.54
32	88.72	69.05	74.91	82.52	80.56	75.93	78.61	55.21	50.05	63.74	54.82	80.92	58.49	60.54
64	88.72	69.05	74.91	82.52	80.56	75.93	78.61	55.21	50.05	63.74	54.82	80.92	58.49	60.54

Table 9: Performance of using different Answer length for generative reader. First block is the result for T5 model and the second block for BART model.

Model	In-domain Datasets							Out-domain Datasets						
	SQuAD	NewsQA	TQA	SQA	HQA	NQ	Avg.	DROP	RACE	BioASQ	TbQA	RE	DuoRC	Avg.
Single Task Learning														
T5 E-Ext (B)	90.12	59.38	67.39	77.14	76.95	75.56	74.42	41.17	45.46	64.92	46.69	84.48	52.61	55.89
T5 E-Ext (L)	92.39	59.62	70.22	78.52	80.06	77.93	76.46	52.73	51.38	69.99	49.76	85.78	54.82	60.74
T5 ED-Ext (B)	90.57	58.00	66.87	77.66	78.68	76.69	74.75	45.49	45.56	66.99	48.66	84.91	51.03	57.11
T5 ED-Gen (B)	90.63	66.74	73.45	82.75	78.81	75.10	77.91	48.07	47.54	67.33	46.19	84.94	43.49	56.26
BART E-Ext (L)	92.15	62.31	72.84	79.99	80.52	78.86	77.78	50.91	48.83	68.18	47.19	86.04	56.89	59.67
BART ED-Ext (L)	92.50	58.81	72.11	80.33	80.30	78.57	77.10	54.74	47.13	66.05	47.00	86.15	54.66	59.29
BART ED-Gen (L)	78.72	63.18	69.22	79.39	72.72	56.09	69.89	44.04	43.64	53.79	38.44	72.17	45.84	49.65
ELECTRA (L)	93.39	60.23	76.31	82.54	80.99	78.78	78.71	55.43	49.80	66.96	47.80	86.23	54.90	60.19
RoBERTa (L)	92.67	59.32	72.52	81.34	80.88	78.82	77.59	55.02	48.18	64.66	52.42	86.65	54.98	60.32
Multi-Task Learning														
T5 E-Ext (B)	90.76$_{+0.64}$	61.69$_{+2.31}$	68.95$_{+1.56}$	77.58$_{+0.44}$	78.63$_{+1.68}$	76.84$_{+1.28}$	75.74$_{+1.32}$	47.25$_{+6.08}$	48.93$_{+3.47}$	66.70$_{+1.78}$	52.23$_{+5.54}$	85.09$_{+0.61}$	53.42$_{+0.81}$	58.94$_{+3.05}$
T5 E-Ext (L)	92.74$_{+0.35}$	60.50$_{+0.88}$	70.50$_{+0.28}$	79.14$_{+0.62}$	81.28$_{+1.22}$	78.44$_{+0.51}$	77.10$_{+0.64}$	58.68$_{+5.95}$	53.07$_{+1.69}$	69.66$_{-0.33}$	55.04$_{+5.28}$	86.53$_{+0.75}$	55.28$_{+0.46}$	63.04$_{+2.30}$
T5 ED-Ext (B)	91.03$_{+0.46}$	60.73$_{+2.73}$	68.80$_{+1.93}$	78.10$_{+0.44}$	79.66$_{+0.98}$	77.19$_{+0.50}$	75.92$_{+1.17}$	48.67$_{+3.18}$	49.06$_{+3.50}$	67.46$_{+0.47}$	50.66$_{+2.00}$	85.49$_{+0.58}$	54.05$_{+3.02}$	59.23$_{+2.12}$
T5 ED-Gen (B)	91.29$_{+0.66}$	66.37$_{-0.37}$	73.99$_{+0.54}$	82.75$_{0.00}$	78.58$_{-0.23}$	75.41$_{+0.31}$	78.06$_{+0.15}$	51.13$_{+3.06}$	48.99$_{+1.45}$	68.65$_{+1.32}$	47.09$_{+0.90}$	85.84$_{+0.90}$	45.23$_{+1.74}$	57.82$_{+1.56}$
BART E-Ext (L)	92.42$_{+0.27}$	61.83$_{-0.48}$	70.98$_{-1.86}$	80.12$_{+0.13}$	82.02$_{+1.50}$	79.13$_{+0.27}$	77.75$_{-0.03}$	58.32$_{+7.41}$	50.06$_{+1.23}$	69.62$_{+1.44}$	55.02$_{+7.83}$	86.79$_{+0.75}$	59.83$_{+2.94}$	63.27$_{+3.60}$
BART ED-Ext (L)	93.06$_{+0.56}$	58.72$_{-0.09}$	70.80$_{-1.31}$	80.11$_{-0.22}$	81.78$_{+1.48}$	79.11$_{+0.54}$	77.26$_{+0.16}$	60.19$_{+5.45}$	48.97$_{+1.84}$	67.47$_{+1.42}$	53.24$_{+6.24}$	86.75$_{+0.60}$	56.22$_{+1.56}$	62.14$_{+2.85}$
BART ED-Gen (L)	88.58$_{+9.86}$	66.18$_{+3.00}$	75.21$_{+5.99}$	83.38$_{+3.99}$	79.88$_{+7.16}$	75.41$_{+19.32}$	78.11$_{+8.22}$	55.07$_{+11.03}$	49.91$_{+6.27}$	63.69$_{+9.90}$	46.75$_{+8.31}$	80.94$_{+8.77}$	48.11$_{+2.27}$	57.41$_{+7.76}$
ELECTRA (L)	93.27$_{-0.12}$	60.59$_{+0.36}$	72.96$_{-3.35}$	82.03$_{-0.51}$	83.10$_{+2.11}$	79.16$_{+0.38}$	78.52$_{-0.19}$	62.56$_{+7.13}$	50.29$_{+0.49}$	71.50$_{+4.54}$	54.60$_{+6.80}$	87.14$_{+0.91}$	56.88$_{+1.98}$	63.83$_{+3.64}$
RoBERTa (L)	93.36$_{+0.69}$	60.15$_{+0.83}$	71.40$_{-1.12}$	80.56$_{-0.78}$	82.21$_{+1.33}$	79.50$_{+0.68}$	77.86$_{+0.27}$	64.79$_{+9.77}$	51.49$_{+3.31}$	68.69$_{+4.03}$	53.68$_{+1.26}$	86.31$_{-0.34}$	57.22$_{+2.24}$	63.70$_{+3.38}$

Table 10: Three readers trained by single and multi task learning and evaluated on in-domain and out-domain datasets by F1 Score. Inference length for all readers is 512.

Model	In-domain Datasets							Out-domain Datasets						
	SQuAD	NewsQA	TQA	SQA	HQA	NQ	Avg.	DROP	RACE	BioASQ	TbQA	RE	DuoRC	Avg.
Single Task Learning														
T5 E-Ext (B)	90.20	69.93	66.26	74.56	77.38	76.44	75.80	41.36	45.63	66.64	54.34	84.48	55.93	58.06
T5 E-Ext (L)	92.47	72.22	70.43	77.10	80.69	79.08	78.67	53.14	52.06	71.26	61.07	85.78	58.72	63.67
T5 ED-Ext (B)	90.71	70.43	68.48	76.01	78.94	77.80	77.06	45.86	46.18	67.93	55.07	84.91	55.19	59.19
T5 ED-Gen (B)	90.75	71.64	79.02	86.09	79.87	76.72	80.68	48.08	48.89	67.36	60.42	84.94	60.83	61.75
BART E-Ext (L)	92.19	72.20	73.12	77.19	80.61	79.29	79.10	51.57	48.82	68.83	51.29	86.04	61.35	61.32
BART ED-Ext (L)	92.51	58.68	72.55	80.94	80.71	78.63	77.34	54.73	47.64	66.15	46.18	86.15	54.39	59.21
BART ED-Gen (L)	78.75	66.20	67.81	78.89	73.22	56.58	70.24	44.22	43.70	55.59	45.11	76.83	55.63	53.51
ELECTRA (L)	93.39	60.23	76.31	82.54	80.99	78.78	78.71	55.43	49.80	66.96	47.80	86.23	54.90	60.19
RoBERTa (L)	92.64	59.95	72.97	81.62	81.21	78.95	77.89	55.88	47.72	64.47	52.31	86.69	55.75	60.47
Multi-Task Learning														
T5 E-Ext (B)	90.81$_{+0.61}$	70.73$_{+0.80}$	66.73$_{+0.47}$	74.96$_{+0.40}$	79.02$_{+1.64}$	77.64$_{+1.20}$	76.65$_{+0.85}$	47.99$_{+6.63}$	49.22$_{+3.59}$	67.59$_{+0.95}$	60.18$_{+5.84}$	85.09$_{+0.61}$	59.24$_{+3.31}$	61.55$_{+3.49}$
T5 E-Ext (L)	92.84$_{+0.37}$	73.15$_{+0.93}$	70.86$_{+0.43}$	77.30$_{+0.20}$	81.88$_{+1.19}$	79.77$_{+0.69}$	79.30$_{+0.63}$	59.10$_{+5.96}$	54.01$_{+1.95}$	71.13$_{-0.13}$	64.63$_{+3.56}$	86.53$_{+0.75}$	61.21$_{+2.49}$	66.10$_{+2.43}$
T5 ED-Ext (B)	91.12$_{+0.41}$	71.78$_{+1.35}$	66.93$_{-1.55}$	76.13$_{+0.12}$	80.23$_{+1.29}$	78.11$_{+0.31}$	77.38$_{+0.32}$	49.69$_{+3.83}$	49.64$_{+3.46}$	68.45$_{+0.52}$	60.50$_{+5.43}$	85.49$_{+0.58}$	57.41$_{+2.22}$	61.86$_{+2.67}$
T5 ED-Gen (B)	91.41$_{+0.66}$	71.27$_{-0.37}$	79.65$_{+0.63}$	86.21$_{+0.12}$	79.70$_{-0.17}$	77.10$_{+0.38}$	80.89$_{+0.21}$	51.20$_{+3.12}$	49.66$_{+0.77}$	68.72$_{+1.36}$	63.02$_{+2.60}$	85.84$_{+0.90}$	62.94$_{+2.11}$	63.56$_{+1.81}$
BART E-Ext (L)	92.46$_{+0.27}$	72.11$_{-0.09}$	72.24$_{-0.88}$	76.53$_{-0.66}$	82.04$_{+1.43}$	79.40$_{+0.11}$	79.13$_{+0.03}$	58.22$_{+6.65}$	50.40$_{+1.58}$	70.72$_{+1.89}$	56.29$_{+5.00}$	86.79$_{+0.75}$	61.95$_{+0.60}$	64.06$_{+2.74}$
BART ED-Ext (L)	93.07$_{+0.56}$	58.67$_{-0.01}$	71.47$_{-1.08}$	80.66$_{-0.28}$	82.14$_{+1.43}$	79.32$_{+0.69}$	77.55$_{+0.21}$	60.40$_{+5.67}$	51.32$_{+3.68}$	67.48$_{+1.33}$	53.34$_{+7.16}$	86.75$_{+0.60}$	56.79$_{+2.40}$	62.68$_{+3.47}$
BART ED-Gen (L)	- 88.63$_{+9.88}$	68.91$_{+2.71}$	74.91$_{+7.10}$	82.52$_{+3.63}$	80.53$_{+7.31}$	75.78$_{+19.20}$	78.55$_{+8.31}$	55.20$_{+10.98}$	50.04$_{+6.34}$	63.78$_{+8.19}$	54.81$_{+9.70}$	80.94$_{+4.11}$	58.47$_{+2.84}$	60.54$_{+7.03}$
ELECTRA (L)	93.27$_{-0.12}$	60.59$_{+0.36}$	72.96$_{-3.35}$	82.03$_{-0.51}$	83.10$_{+2.11}$	79.16$_{+0.38}$	78.52$_{-0.19}$	62.56$_{+7.13}$	50.29$_{+0.49}$	71.50$_{+4.54}$	54.60$_{+6.80}$	87.14$_{+0.91}$	56.88$_{+1.98}$	63.83$_{+3.64}$
RoBERTa (L)	93.41$_{+0.77}$	59.56$_{-0.39}$	72.23$_{-0.74}$	80.98$_{-0.64}$	82.37$_{+1.16}$	79.55$_{+0.60}$	78.02$_{+0.13}$	64.47$_{+8.59}$	51.81$_{+4.09}$	69.15$_{+4.68}$	53.68$_{+1.37}$	86.31$_{-0.38}$	56.06$_{+0.31}$	63.58$_{+3.11}$

Table 11: Three readers trained by single and multi task learning and evaluated on in-domain and out-domain datasets by F1 Score. Inference length for all readers is 1024, except for ELECTRA is 512.

Model	In-domain Datasets							Out-of-domain Datasets						
	SQuAD	NewsQA	TQA	SQA	HQA	NQ	Avg.	DROP	RACE	BioASQ	TbQA	RE	DuoRC	Avg.
Single Task Learning														
T5 E-Ext (B)	90.20	70.14	72.67	79.89	77.37	77.31	77.93	41.36	45.63	66.64	55.17	84.48	58.62	58.65
T5 E-Ext (L)	92.47	72.63	76.09	83.24	80.67	80.00	80.85	53.14	52.06	71.26	61.92	85.78	62.80	64.49
T5 ED-Ext (B)	90.71	70.80	74.16	81.32	78.98	78.68	79.11	45.86	46.18	67.93	55.74	84.91	59.33	59.99
T5 ED-Gen (B)	90.75	71.65	79.61	86.21	79.89	78.04	81.02	48.08	48.89	67.36	60.30	84.94	61.35	61.82
BART E-Ext (L)	92.19	72.20	73.12	77.19	80.61	79.29	79.10	51.57	48.82	68.83	51.29	86.04	61.35	61.32
BART ED-Ext (L)	92.51	58.68	72.55	80.94	80.71	78.63	77.34	54.73	47.64	66.15	46.18	86.15	54.39	59.21
BART ED-Gen (L)	78.75	66.20	67.81	78.89	73.22	56.58	70.24	44.22	43.70	55.59	45.11	76.83	55.63	53.51
ELECTRA (L)	93.39	60.23	76.31	82.54	80.99	78.78	78.71	55.43	49.80	66.96	47.80	86.23	54.90	60.19
RoBERTa (L)	92.64	59.95	72.97	81.62	81.21	78.95	77.89	55.88	47.72	64.47	52.31	86.69	55.75	60.47
Multi-Task Learning														
T5 E-Ext (B)	90.81$_{+0.61}$	70.92$_{+0.78}$	74.22$_{+1.55}$	80.42$_{+0.53}$	79.03$_{+1.66}$	78.57$_{+1.26}$	78.99$_{+1.06}$	47.99$_{+6.63}$	49.22$_{+3.59}$	67.59$_{+0.95}$	60.52$_{+5.35}$	85.09$_{+0.61}$	61.44$_{+2.82}$	61.98$_{+3.33}$
T5 E-Ext (L)	92.84$_{+0.37}$	73.51$_{+0.88}$	77.37$_{+1.28}$	82.89$_{-0.35}$	81.92$_{+1.25}$	80.74$_{+0.74}$	81.55$_{+0.70}$	59.10$_{+5.96}$	54.01$_{+1.95}$	71.13$_{-0.13}$	64.90$_{+2.98}$	86.53$_{+0.75}$	65.01$_{+2.21}$	66.78$_{+2.29}$
T5 ED-Ext (B)	91.12$_{+0.41}$	71.95$_{+1.15}$	75.50$_{+1.34}$	81.82$_{+0.50}$	80.25$_{+1.27}$	78.93$_{+0.25}$	79.93$_{+0.82}$	49.69$_{+3.83}$	49.64$_{+3.46}$	68.45$_{+0.52}$	61.33$_{+5.59}$	85.49$_{+0.58}$	61.22$_{+1.89}$	62.64$_{+2.65}$
T5 ED-Gen (L)	91.41$_{+0.66}$	71.29$_{-0.36}$	80.01$_{+0.40}$	86.46$_{+0.25}$	79.70$_{-0.19}$	78.09$_{+0.05}$	81.16$_{+0.14}$	51.20$_{+3.12}$	49.66$_{+0.77}$	68.72$_{+1.36}$	62.90$_{+2.60}$	85.84$_{+0.90}$	63.76$_{+2.41}$	63.68$_{+1.86}$
BART E-Ext (L)	92.46$_{+0.27}$	72.11$_{-0.09}$	72.24$_{-0.88}$	76.53$_{-0.66}$	82.04$_{+1.43}$	79.40$_{+0.11}$	79.13$_{+0.03}$	58.22$_{+6.65}$	50.40$_{+1.58}$	70.72$_{+1.89}$	56.29$_{+5.00}$	86.79$_{+0.75}$	61.95$_{+0.60}$	64.06$_{+2.74}$
BART ED-Ext (L)	93.07$_{+0.56}$	58.67$_{-0.01}$	71.47$_{-1.08}$	80.66$_{-0.25}$	82.14$_{+1.43}$	79.32$_{+0.69}$	77.55$_{+0.21}$	60.40$_{+5.67}$	51.32$_{+3.68}$	67.48$_{+1.33}$	53.34$_{+7.16}$	86.75$_{+0.60}$	56.79$_{+2.40}$	62.68$_{+3.47}$
BART ED-Gen (L)	88.63$_{+9.88}$	68.91$_{+2.71}$	74.91$_{+7.10}$	82.52$_{+3.63}$	80.53$_{+7.31}$	75.78$_{+19.20}$	78.55$_{+8.31}$	55.20$_{+10.98}$	50.04$_{+6.34}$	63.78$_{+8.19}$	54.81$_{+9.70}$	80.94$_{+4.11}$	58.47$_{+2.84}$	60.54$_{+7.03}$
ELECTRA (L)	93.27$_{-0.12}$	60.59$_{+0.36}$	72.96$_{-3.35}$	82.03$_{-0.51}$	83.10$_{+2.11}$	79.16$_{+0.38}$	78.52$_{-0.19}$	62.56$_{+7.13}$	50.29$_{+0.49}$	71.50$_{+4.54}$	54.60$_{+6.80}$	87.14$_{+0.91}$	56.88$_{+1.98}$	63.83$_{+3.64}$
RoBERTa (L)	93.41$_{+0.77}$	59.56$_{-0.39}$	72.23$_{-0.74}$	80.98$_{-0.64}$	82.37$_{+1.16}$	79.55$_{+0.60}$	78.02$_{+0.13}$	64.47$_{+8.59}$	51.81$_{+4.09}$	69.15$_{+4.68}$	53.68$_{+1.37}$	86.31$_{-0.38}$	56.06$_{+0.31}$	63.58$_{+3.11}$

Table 12: Three readers trained by single and multi task learning and evaluated on in-domain and out-domain datasets by F1 Score. Inference length for T5 readers is full length, for BART is 1024, and for ELECTRA is 512.

Model	In-domain Datasets							Out-of-domain Datasets						
	SQuAD	NewsQA	TQA	SQA	HQA	NQ	Avg.	DROP	RACE	BioASQ	TbQA	RE	DuoRC	Avg.
Single Task Learning														
T5 E-Ext (B)	90.20	70.14	72.67	79.89	77.37	77.31	77.93	41.36	45.63	66.64	55.17	84.48	58.62	58.65
T5 ED-Ext (B)	90.71	70.80	74.16	81.32	78.98	78.68	79.11	45.86	46.18	67.93	55.74	84.91	59.33	59.99
T5 ED-Gen (B)	90.75	71.65	79.61	86.21	79.89	78.04	81.02	48.08	48.89	67.36	60.30	84.94	61.35	61.82
BART E-Ext (L)	92.19	72.20	73.12	77.19	80.61	79.29	79.10	51.57	48.82	68.83	51.29	86.04	61.35	61.32
BART ED-Ext	92.51	58.68	72.55	80.94	80.71	78.63	77.34	54.73	47.64	66.15	46.18	86.15	54.39	59.21
BART ED-Gen (L)	78.75	66.20	67.81	78.89	73.22	56.58	70.24	44.22	43.70	55.59	45.11	76.83	55.63	53.51
Multi-Task Learning														
T5 E-Ext (B)	$90.81_{+0.61}$	$70.92_{+0.78}$	$74.22_{+1.55}$	$80.42_{+0.53}$	$79.03_{+1.66}$	$78.57_{+1.26}$	$78.99_{+1.06}$	$47.99_{+6.63}$	$49.22_{+3.59}$	$67.59_{+0.95}$	$60.52_{+5.35}$	$85.09_{+0.61}$	$61.44_{+2.82}$	$61.98_{+3.33}$
T5 ED-Ext (B)	$91.12_{+0.41}$	$71.95_{+1.15}$	$75.50_{+1.34}$	$81.82_{+0.50}$	$80.25_{+1.27}$	$78.93_{+0.25}$	$79.93_{+0.82}$	$49.69_{+3.83}$	$49.64_{+3.46}$	$68.45_{+0.52}$	$61.33_{+5.59}$	$85.49_{+0.58}$	$61.22_{+1.89}$	$62.64_{+2.65}$
T5 ED-Gen (L)	$91.41_{+0.66}$	$71.29_{-0.36}$	$80.01_{+0.40}$	$86.46_{+0.25}$	$79.70_{-0.19}$	$78.09_{+0.05}$	$81.16_{+0.14}$	$51.20_{+3.12}$	$49.66_{+0.77}$	$68.72_{+1.36}$	$62.90_{+2.60}$	$85.84_{+0.90}$	$63.76_{+2.41}$	$63.68_{+1.86}$
BART E-Ext (L)	$92.46_{+0.27}$	$72.11_{-0.09}$	$72.24_{-0.88}$	$76.53_{-0.66}$	$82.04_{+1.43}$	$79.40_{+0.11}$	$79.13_{+0.03}$	$58.22_{+6.65}$	$50.40_{+1.58}$	$70.72_{+1.89}$	$56.29_{+5.00}$	$86.79_{+0.75}$	$61.95_{+0.60}$	$64.06_{+2.74}$
BART ED-Ext (L)	$93.07_{+0.56}$	$58.67_{-0.01}$	$71.47_{-1.08}$	$80.66_{-0.28}$	$82.14_{+1.43}$	$79.32_{+0.69}$	$77.55_{+0.21}$	$60.40_{+5.67}$	$51.32_{+3.68}$	$67.48_{+1.33}$	$53.34_{+7.16}$	$86.75_{+0.60}$	$56.79_{+2.40}$	$62.68_{+3.47}$
BART ED-Gen (L)	$88.63_{+9.88}$	$68.91_{+2.71}$	$74.91_{+7.10}$	$82.52_{+3.63}$	$80.53_{+7.31}$	$75.78_{+19.20}$	$78.55_{+8.31}$	$55.20_{+10.98}$	$50.04_{+6.34}$	$63.78_{+8.19}$	$54.81_{+9.70}$	$80.94_{+4.11}$	$58.47_{+2.84}$	$60.54_{+7.03}$

Table 13: Comparison of readers based on the same PrLMs by F1 Score. For three T5 readers, we use the T5-base model, for three BART readers, we use the BART-large model. Avg. means the Macro Average of in/out-domain datasets. Inference length for T5 is full length of context, for ELECTRA is 512 and for BART and RoBERTa is 1024.

Model	Test / Train	In-domain Datasets						Out-domain Datasets					
		SQuAD	NewsQA	TQA	SQA	HQA	NQ	DROP	RACE	BioASQ	TbQA	RE	DuoRC
Single Task Learning													
T5 E-Ext (B)	SQuAD	90.20	63.37	63.75	30.97	67.53	62.28	36.03	45.63	66.38	54.77	84.48	57.08
	NewsQA	84.54	70.14	63.99	42.32	61.55	63.50	23.48	44.07	62.13	50.25	77.59	58.62
	TQA	69.68	46.83	72.67	60.40	54.33	54.49	24.28	37.15	60.07	42.61	75.83	47.72
	SQA	60.75	40.49	68.37	79.89	44.21	49.84	23.68	30.02	55.93	39.28	75.26	43.36
	HQA	83.30	59.19	61.67	48.18	77.37	62.35	39.04	40.51	63.68	40.15	84.07	55.31
	NQ	83.87	60.81	65.64	52.24	64.60	77.31	41.36	43.99	66.64	55.17	82.58	52.88
T5 E-Ext (L)	SQuAD	92.47	65.33	67.97	32.73	71.00	64.97	52.01	50.13	68.66	53.03	85.78	61.41
	NewsQA	87.38	72.63	69.34	43.83	66.56	69.02	31.72	49.72	65.97	55.51	78.75	62.80
	TQA	74.97	50.27	76.09	63.26	57.26	58.68	40.09	38.55	65.95	52.34	81.01	55.21
	SQA	72.47	48.12	73.57	83.24	53.50	57.17	41.57	35.53	66.07	52.64	81.63	52.05
	HQA	86.88	62.42	66.16	46.47	80.67	67.13	47.43	45.10	68.27	51.37	84.89	56.80
	NQ	86.73	64.62	70.32	54.09	68.54	80.00	53.14	52.06	71.26	61.92	84.35	60.43
T5 ED-Ext (B)	SQuAD	92.47	65.33	67.97	32.73	71.00	64.97	52.01	50.13	68.66	53.03	85.78	61.41
	NewsQA	87.38	72.63	69.34	43.83	66.56	69.02	31.72	49.72	65.97	55.51	78.75	62.80
	TQA	74.97	50.27	76.09	63.26	57.26	58.68	40.09	38.55	65.95	52.34	81.01	55.21
	SQA	72.47	48.12	73.57	83.24	53.50	57.17	41.57	35.53	66.07	52.64	81.63	52.05
	HQA	86.88	62.42	66.16	46.47	80.67	67.13	47.43	45.10	68.27	51.37	84.89	56.80
	NQ	86.73	64.62	70.32	54.09	68.54	80.00	53.14	52.06	71.26	61.92	84.35	60.43
T5 ED-Gen (B)	SQuAD	90.75	60.51	69.56	24.11	68.57	57.19	43.31	48.89	65.96	46.75	84.94	60.31
	NewsQA	85.75	71.65	69.70	43.16	63.61	62.96	25.37	45.97	62.80	53.82	77.37	61.35
	TQA	74.33	49.26	79.61	57.14	58.75	55.18	33.84	42.38	56.94	51.16	80.52	52.69
	SQA	70.62	44.66	78.03	86.21	57.19	52.92	35.32	35.33	59.76	53.66	79.54	49.23
	HQA	86.24	60.25	70.57	51.23	79.89	62.33	44.94	46.38	66.93	42.65	84.56	59.60
	NQ	85.46	61.80	72.08	57.55	67.71	78.04	48.08	45.85	67.36	60.30	84.06	58.42
BART E-Ext (L)	SQuAD	92.19	62.30	60.86	35.52	69.60	62.94	51.31	48.82	68.83	49.39	86.04	58.31
	NewsQA	85.04	72.20	62.86	41.17	61.81	65.84	31.99	48.82	61.98	49.29	77.30	61.35
	TQA	68.36	43.38	73.12	55.53	59.27	55.11	37.79	36.16	53.90	37.98	80.07	49.51
	SQA	50.74	31.48	66.74	77.19	40.65	43.53	22.15	23.90	53.76	36.38	66.48	37.12
	HQA	82.21	52.46	56.53	34.95	80.61	62.58	44.30	39.60	59.40	33.74	85.46	52.60
	NQ	83.12	59.44	62.12	49.19	62.73	79.29	51.57	43.23	64.77	51.29	83.13	54.63
BART ED-Ext (L)	SQuAD	92.51	53.70	62.64	41.85	67.69	60.82	54.73	47.64	66.15	46.18	86.15	54.39
	NewsQA	86.15	58.68	62.29	46.98	64.09	66.00	31.91	45.52	60.70	44.82	78.72	54.09
	TQA	69.82	38.40	72.55	61.02	61.05	54.10	34.63	36.36	54.34	39.35	81.28	46.43
	SQA	57.26	32.09	69.35	80.94	41.82	45.62	28.54	25.18	51.50	41.09	70.98	38.88
	HQA	83.29	49.66	63.18	40.46	80.71	63.52	47.91	38.56	59.78	34.60	84.32	52.04
	NQ	83.86	50.35	64.06	56.34	62.53	78.63	52.41	44.25	65.59	45.93	84.43	49.44
BART ED-Gen (L)	SQuAD	78.75	54.02	48.69	22.33	57.19	57.90	44.09	41.33	47.04	35.42	70.68	45.79
	NewsQA	78.65	66.20	58.02	36.31	57.91	61.10	28.36	43.70	53.71	45.11	72.17	55.63
	TQA	58.98	39.22	67.81	53.90	54.81	46.73	32.85	33.74	46.62	39.97	64.89	45.47
	SQA	40.51	28.33	65.42	78.89	37.05	36.12	23.45	22.42	46.71	39.43	52.23	38.24
	HQA	74.75	50.41	56.56	40.90	73.22	57.83	44.22	37.31	55.59	29.96	76.83	50.62
	NQ	61.09	39.05	38.21	33.48	43.59	56.58	40.27	32.01	51.24	36.63	59.46	33.69
RoBERTa (L)	SQuAD	92.64	54.76	65.90	45.76	71.35	59.43	52.51	47.13	64.47	52.31	86.69	55.75
	NewsQA	86.50	59.95	63.01	48.02	66.99	67.29	33.52	47.26	60.05	45.10	78.08	54.27
	TQA	73.63	41.05	72.97	51.16	62.44	55.76	44.40	39.27	54.92	42.72	82.32	49.89
	SQA	53.59	29.57	70.35	81.62	42.03	47.06	23.04	23.70	54.18	39.69	71.13	36.06
	HQA	85.10	50.55	65.06	44.31	81.21	63.88	51.74	36.86	62.44	37.49	85.07	54.02
	NQ	85.25	49.49	64.48	57.23	67.47	78.95	55.88	47.72	63.77	44.67	84.10	50.00
ELECTRA (L)	SQuAD	93.39	55.42	65.92	46.56	68.69	68.92	55.11	49.80	66.96	46.57	86.23	54.90
	NewsQA	86.33	60.23	65.13	49.39	63.97	68.03	30.74	46.45	64.86	46.79	78.21	53.78
	TQA	69.75	40.20	76.31	65.27	58.87	55.95	42.21	37.46	59.94	41.54	80.56	49.24
	SQA	52.17	28.21	71.39	82.54	44.81	43.28	36.68	22.47	58.35	42.76	69.54	39.16
	HQA	84.43	51.23	65.83	50.25	80.99	64.89	48.91	38.24	65.77	36.53	83.86	50.50
	NQ	85.45	50.81	66.65	62.88	64.00	78.78	55.43	47.29	66.39	47.80	83.43	51.15
Multi-Task Learning													
T5 E-Ext (B)	Multi	90.81	70.92	74.22	80.42	79.03	78.57	47.99	49.22	67.59	60.52	85.09	61.44
T5 E-Ext (L)	Multi	92.84	73.51	77.37	82.89	81.92	80.74	59.10	54.01	71.13	64.90	86.53	65.01
T5 ED-Ext (B)	Multi	91.12	71.95	75.50	81.82	80.25	78.93	49.69	49.64	68.45	61.33	85.49	61.22
T5 ED-Gen (B)	Multi	91.41	71.29	80.01	86.46	79.70	78.09	51.20	49.66	68.72	62.90	85.84	63.76
BART E-Ext (L)	Multi	92.46	72.11	72.24	76.53	82.04	79.40	58.22	50.40	70.72	56.29	86.79	61.95
BART ED-Ext (L)	Multi	93.07	58.67	71.47	80.66	82.14	79.32	60.40	51.32	67.48	53.34	86.75	56.79
BART ED-Gen (L)	Multi	88.63	68.91	74.91	82.52	80.53	75.78	55.20	50.04	63.78	54.81	80.94	58.47
RoBERTa (L)	93.41	59.56	72.23	80.98	82.37	79.55	64.47	51.81	69.15	53.68	86.31	56.06	
ELECTRA (L)	Multi	93.27	60.59	72.96	82.03	83.10	79.16	62.56	50.29	71.50	54.60	87.14	56.88

Table 14: Evaluation by F1 score. TQA: TriviaQA; SQA:SearchQA; HQA:HotpotQA; NQ: NaturalQuestions; TbQA:TextbookQA; RE:RelationExtraction. For inference length, T5 use Full length, BART and RoBERTa use 1024 and ELECTRA use 512.

Efficient Machine Translation Domain Adaptation

Pedro Henrique Martins[Ψ] **Zita Marinho**[ᗫ,ᗰ] **André F. T. Martins**[Ψ,♀,ƀ]
[Ψ]Instituto de Telecomunicações [ᗫ]DeepMind [ᗰ]Institute of Systems and Robotics
[♀]LUMLIS (Lisbon ELLIS Unit), Instituto Superior Técnico [ƀ]Unbabel
Lisbon, Portugal
pedrohenriqueamartins@tecnico.ulisboa.pt,
zmarinho@google.com, andre.t.martins@tecnico.ulisboa.pt.

Abstract

Machine translation models struggle when translating out-of-domain text, which makes domain adaptation a topic of critical importance. However, most domain adaptation methods focus on fine-tuning or training the entire or part of the model on every new domain, which can be costly. On the other hand, semi-parametric models have been shown to successfully perform domain adaptation by retrieving examples from an in-domain datastore (Khandelwal et al., 2021). A drawback of these retrieval-augmented models, however, is that they tend to be substantially slower. In this paper, we explore several approaches to speed up nearest neighbor machine translation. We adapt the methods recently proposed by He et al. (2021) for language modeling, and introduce a simple but effective caching strategy that avoids performing retrieval when similar contexts have been seen before. Translation quality and runtimes for several domains show the effectiveness of the proposed solutions.[1]

1 Introduction

Modern neural machine translation models are mostly parametric (Bahdanau et al., 2015; Vaswani et al., 2017), meaning that, for each input, the output depends only on a fixed number of model parameters, obtained using some training data, hopefully in the same domain. However, when running machine translation systems in the wild, it is often the case that the model is given input sentences or documents from domains that were not part of the training data, which frequently leads to subpar translations. One solution is training or fine-tuning the entire model or just part of it for each domain, but this can be expensive and may lead to catastrophic forgetting (Saunders, 2021).

Recently, an approach that has achieved promising results is augmenting parametric models with a retrieval component, leading to *semi-parametric* models (Gu et al., 2018; Zhang et al., 2018; Bapna and Firat, 2019; Khandelwal et al., 2021; Meng et al., 2021; Zheng et al., 2021; Jiang et al., 2021). These models construct a datastore based on a set of source / target sentences or word-level contexts (translation memories) and retrieve similar examples from this datastore, using this information in the generation process. This allows having only one model that can be used for every domain. However, the model's runtime increases with the size of the domain's datastore and searching for related examples on large datastores can be computationally very expensive: for example, when retrieving 64 neighbors from the datastore, the model may become two orders of magnitude slower (Khandelwal et al., 2021). Due to this, some recent works have proposed methods that aim to make this process more efficient. Meng et al. (2021) proposed constructing a different datastore for each source sentence, by first searching for the neighbors of the source tokens; and He et al. (2021) proposed several techniques – datastore pruning, adaptive retrieval, dimension reduction – for nearest neighbor language modeling.

In this paper, we adapt several methods proposed by He et al. (2021) to machine translation, and we further propose a new approach that increases the model's efficiency: the use of a retrieval distributions cache. By caching the kNN probability distributions, together with the corresponding decoder representations, for the previous steps of the generation of the current translation(s), the model can quickly retrieve the retrieval distribution when the current representation is similar to a cached one, instead of having to search for neighbors in the datastore at every single step.

We perform a thorough analysis of the model's efficiency on a controlled setting, which shows that the combination of our proposed techniques results in a model, the efficient kNN-MT, which is approx-

[1]The code is available at https://github.com/deep-spin/efficient_kNN_MT.

Proceedings of the 1st Workshop on Semiparametric Methods in NLP: Decoupling Logic from Knowledge, pages 23 - 29
May 27, 2022 ©2022 Association for Computational Linguistics

imately twice as fast as the vanilla kNN-MT. This comes without harming translation performance, which is, on average, more than 8 BLEU points and 5 COMET points better than the base MT model.

In sum, this paper presents the following contributions:

- We adapt the methods proposed by He et al. (2021) for efficient nearest neighbor language modeling to machine translation.
- We propose a caching strategy to store the retrieval probability distributions, improving the translation speed.
- We compare the efficiency and translation quality of the different methods, which show the benefits of the proposed and adapted techniques.

2 Background

When performing machine translation, the model is given a source sentence or document, $\boldsymbol{x} = [x_1, \ldots, x_L]$, on one language, and the goal is to output a translation of the sentence in the desired language, $\boldsymbol{y} = [y_1, \ldots, y_N]$. This is usually done using a parametric sequence-to-sequence model (Bahdanau et al., 2015; Vaswani et al., 2017), in which the encoder receives the source sentence as input and outputs a set of hidden states. Then, at each step t, the decoder attends to these hidden states and outputs a probability distribution $p_{\text{NMT}}(y_t|\boldsymbol{y}_{<t}, \boldsymbol{x})$ over the vocabulary. Finally, these probability distributions are used to predict the output tokens, typically with beam search.

2.1 Nearest Neighbor Machine Translation

Khandelwal et al. (2021) introduced a nearest neighbor machine translation model, kNN-MT, which is a semi-parametric model. This means that besides having a parametric component that outputs a probability distribution over the vocabulary, $p_{\text{NMT}}(y_t|\boldsymbol{y}_{<t}, \boldsymbol{x})$, the model also has a nearest neighbor retrieval mechanism, which allows direct access to a datastore of examples.

More specifically, we build a datastore $\mathcal{D}$ which consists of a key-value memory, where each entry key is the decoder's output representation, $\boldsymbol{f}(\boldsymbol{x}, \boldsymbol{y}_{<t})$, and the value is the target token y_t:

$$\mathcal{D} = \{(\boldsymbol{f}(\boldsymbol{x}, \boldsymbol{y}_{<t}), y_t) \; \forall y_t \in \boldsymbol{y} \mid (\boldsymbol{x}, \boldsymbol{y}) \in (\mathcal{X}, \mathcal{Y})\}, \tag{1}$$

where $(\mathcal{X}, \mathcal{Y})$ corresponds to a set of parallel source and target sequences. Then, at inference time, the model searches the datastore to retrieve the set of k nearest neighbors $\mathcal{N}$. Using their distances $d(\cdot)$ to the current decoder's output representation, we can compute the retrieval distribution $p_{k\text{NN}}(y_t|\boldsymbol{y}_{<t}, \boldsymbol{x})$ as:

$$p_{k\text{NN}}(y_t|\boldsymbol{y}_{<t}, \boldsymbol{x}) = \frac{\sum_{(\boldsymbol{k}_j, v_j) \in \mathcal{N}} \mathbb{1}_{y_t = v_j} \exp\left(-d\left(\boldsymbol{k}_j, \boldsymbol{f}(\boldsymbol{x}, \boldsymbol{y}_{<t})\right)/T\right)}{\sum_{(\boldsymbol{k}_j, v_j) \in \mathcal{N}} \exp\left(-d\left(\boldsymbol{k}_j, \boldsymbol{f}(\boldsymbol{x}, \boldsymbol{y}_{<t})\right)/T\right)}, \tag{2}$$

where T is the softmax temperature, k_j denotes the key of the jth neighbor and v_j its value. Finally, $p_{\text{NMT}}(y_t|\boldsymbol{y}_{<t}, \boldsymbol{x})$ and $p_{k\text{NN}}(y_t|\boldsymbol{y}_{<t}, \boldsymbol{x})$ are combined to obtain the final distribution, which is used to generate the translation through beam search, by performing interpolation:

$$\begin{aligned} p(y_t|\boldsymbol{y}_{<t}, \boldsymbol{x}) =& (1-\lambda)\, p_{\text{NMT}}(y_t|\boldsymbol{y}_{<t}, \boldsymbol{x}) \\ &+ \lambda\, p_{k\text{NN}}(y_t|\boldsymbol{y}_{<t}, \boldsymbol{x}), \end{aligned} \tag{3}$$

where λ is a hyper-parameter that controls the weights given to the two distributions.

3 Efficient kNN-MT

In this section, we describe the approaches introduced by He et al. (2021) to speed-up the inference time for nearest neighbor language modeling, such as pruning the datastore (§3.1) and reducing the representations dimension (§3.2), which we adapt to machine translation. We further describe a novel method that allows the model to have access to examples without having to search them in the datastore at every step, by maintaining a cache of the past retrieval distributions, for the current translation(s) (§3.3).

3.1 Datastore Pruning

The goal of datastore pruning is to reduce the size of the datastore, so that the model is able to search for the nearest neighbors faster, without severely compromising the translation performance. To do so, we follow He et al. (2021), and use greedy merging. In greedy merging, we aim to merge datastore entries that share the same value (target token) while their keys are close to each other in vector space. To do this, we first need to find the k nearest neighbors of every entry of the datastore, where k is a hyper-parameter. Then, if in the set of neighbors, retrieved for a given entry, there is an entry which has not been merged before and has the same value, we merge the two entries, by simply removing the neighboring one.

3.2 Dimension Reduction

The decoder's output representations, $\boldsymbol{f}(\boldsymbol{x}, \boldsymbol{y}_{<t})$ are, usually, high-dimensional (1024, in our case). This leads to a high computational cost when computing vector distances, which are needed for retrieving neighbors from the datastore. To alleviate this, we follow He et al. (2021), and use principal component analysis (PCA), an efficient dimension reduction method, to reduce the dimension of the decoder's output representation to a pre-defined dimension, d, and generate a compressed datastore.

3.3 Cache

The model does not need to search the datastore at every step of the translation generation in order to do it correctly. Here, we aim to predict when it needs to retrieve neighbors from the datastore, so that, by only searching the datastore in the necessary steps, we can increase the generation speed.

Adaptive retrieval. To do so, first we follow He et al. (2021), and use a simple MLP to predict the value of the interpolation coefficient λ at each step. Then, we define a threshold, α, so that the model only performs retrieval when $\lambda > \alpha$. However, we observed that this leads to results (§A.3) similar to randomly selecting when to search the datastore. We posit that this occurs because it is difficult to predict when the model should perform retrieval, for domain adaptation (He et al., 2021), and because in machine translation error propagation occurs more prominently than in language modeling.

Cache. Because it is common to have similar contexts along the generation process, when using beam search, the model can be often retrieving similar neighbors at different steps, which is not efficient. To avoid repeating searches on the datastore for similar context vectors, $\boldsymbol{f}(\boldsymbol{x}, \boldsymbol{y}_{<t})$, we propose keeping a cache of the previous retrieval distributions, of the current translation(s). More specifically, at each step of the generation of $\boldsymbol{y}$, we add the decoder's representation vector along with the retrieval distribution $p_{k\mathrm{NN}}(y_t|\boldsymbol{y}_{<t}, \boldsymbol{x})$, corresponding to all beams, $\mathcal{B}$, to the cache $\mathcal{C}$:

$$\mathcal{C}=\{(\boldsymbol{f}(\boldsymbol{x}, \boldsymbol{y}_{<t}), p_{k\mathrm{NN}}(y_t|\boldsymbol{y}_{<t},\boldsymbol{x}))\forall y_t \in \boldsymbol{y} \,|\, \boldsymbol{y} \in \mathcal{B}\}. \quad (4)$$

Then, at each step of the generation, we compute the Euclidean distance between the current decoder's representation and the keys on the cache. If all distances are bigger than a threshold τ, the model searches the datastore to find the nearest neighbors. Otherwise, the model retrieves, from the cache, the retrieval distribution that corresponds to the closest key.

4 Experiments

Dataset and metrics. We perform experiments on the Medical, Law, IT, and Koran domain data of the multi-domains dataset (Koehn and Knowles, 2017) re-splitted by Aharoni and Goldberg (2020). To build the datastores we use the in-domain training sets which have from 17,982 to 467,309 sentences. The validation and test sets have 2,000 sentences.

To evaluate the models we use BLEU (Papineni et al., 2002; Post, 2018) and COMET (Rei et al., 2020).

Settings. We use the WMT'19 German-English news translation task winner (Ng et al., 2019) (with 269 M parameters), available on the Fairseq library (Ott et al., 2019), as the base MT model.

As baselines, we consider the base MT model, the vanilla kNN-MT model (Khandelwal et al., 2021), and the Fast kNN-MT model (Meng et al., 2021). For all models, which perform retrieval, we select the hyper-parameters, for each method and each domain, by performing grid search on $k \in \{8, 16, 32, 64\}$ and $\lambda \in \{0.5, 0.6, 0.7, 0.8\}$. The selected values are stated in Table 9 of App. B.

For the vanilla kNN-MT model and the efficient kNN-MT we follow Khandelwal et al. (2021) and use the Euclidean distance to perform retrieval and the proposed softmax temperature. For the Fast kNN-MT, we use the cosine distance and the softmax temperature proposed by Meng et al. (2021). For the efficient kNN-MT we selected parameters that ensure a good speed/quality trade-off: $k = 2$ for datastore pruning, $d = 256$ for PCA, and $\tau = 6$ as the cache threshold. Results for each methods using different parameters are reported in App. A.

4.1 Results

The translation scores are reported on Table 1. We can clearly see that both Fast kNN-MT and the efficient kNN-MT (combining the different methods) do not hurt the translation performance substantially, still leading to, on average, 8 BLEU

	BLEU					COMET				
	Medical	Law	IT	Koran	Average	Medical	Law	IT	Koran	Average
Baselines										
Base MT	40.01	45.64	37.91	16.35	34.98	.4702	.5770	.3942	-.0097	.3579
kNN-MT	54.47	61.23	45.96	21.02	45.67	.5760	.6781	.5163	.0480	.4546
Fast kNN-MT	52.90	55.71	44.73	21.29	43.66	.5293	.5944	.5445	-.0455	.4057
Efficient kNN-MT										
cache	53.30	59.12	45.39	20.67	44.62	.5625	.6403	.5085	.0346	.4365
PCA + cache	53.58	58.57	46.29	20.67	44.78	.5457	.6379	.5311	-.0021	.4282
PCA + pruning	53.23	60.38	45.16	20.52	44.82	.5658	.6639	.4981	.0298	.4394
PCA + cache + pruning	51.90	57.82	44.44	20.11	43.57	.5513	.6260	.4909	-.0052	.4158

Table 1: BLEU and COMET scores on the multi-domains test set, for a batch size of 8.

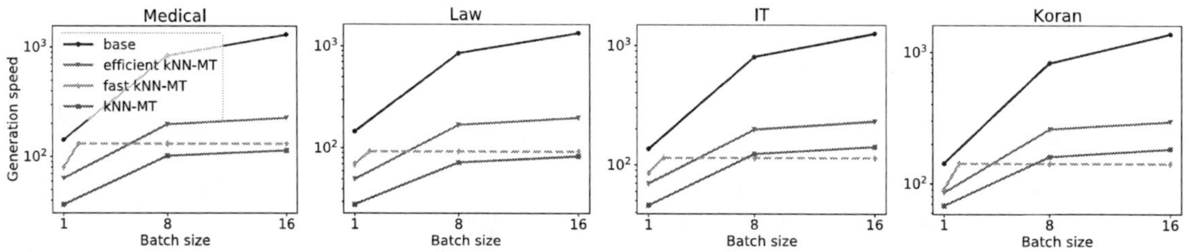

Figure 1: Plots of the generation speed (tokens/s) for the different models on the medical, law, IT, and Koran domains, for different batch sizes (1,8,16). The generation speed (y-axis) is in log scale. When using the Fast kNN-MT model, the maximum batch size that we are able to use is 2, due to out of memory errors.

points and 5 COMET points more than the base MT model.

4.2 Generation speed

Computational infrastructure. All experiments were performed on a server with 3 RTX 2080 Ti (11 GB), 12 AMD Ryzen 2920X CPUs (24 cores), and 128 Gb of RAM. For the generation speed measurements, we ran each model on a single GPU while no other process was running on the server, to have a controlled environment. To search the datastore, we used the FAISS library (Johnson et al., 2019). When using the vanilla kNN-MT and efficient kNN-MT, the nearest neighbor search is performed on the CPUs, since not all datastores fit into memory, while when using the Fast kNN-MT this is done on the GPU.

Analysis. As can be seen on the plots of Figure 1, for a batch size of 1 Fast kNN-MT leads to a generation speed higher than our proposed method and vanilla kNN-MT. However, because of its high memory requirements, we are not able to run Fast kNN-MT for batch sizes larger than 2, on the computational infrastructure stated above. On the contrary, when using the proposed methods (efficient kNN-MT) we are able to run the model with higher batch sizes, achieving superior generation speeds to Fast kNN-MT and vanilla kNN-MT, and reducing the gap to the base MT model.

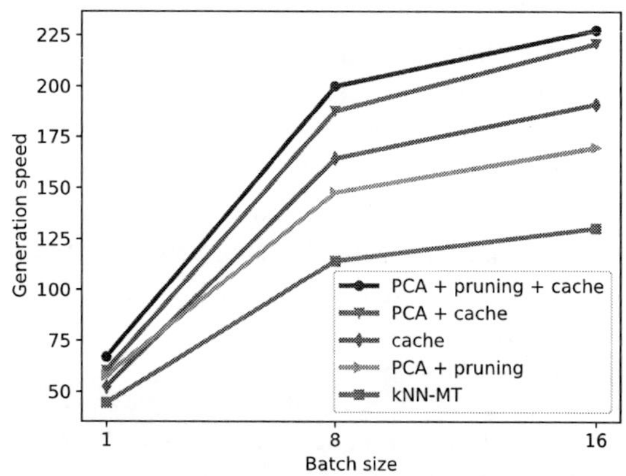

Figure 2: Plot of the generation speed (tokens/s), averaged across domains, for different combinations of the proposed methods.

Ablation. We plot the generation speed for different combinations of the proposed methods (averaged across domains), for several batch sizes, on Figure 2. On this plot, we can clearly see that every method contributes to the speed-up achieved by the model that combines all approaches. Moreover, we can observe that the method which leads to the largest speed-up is the use of a cache of retrieval distributions, by saving, on average 57% of the retrieval searches.

5 Conclusion

In this paper we propose the efficient kNN-MT, in which we combine several methods to improve the kNN-MT generation speed. First, we adapted to machine translation methods that improve retrieval efficiency in language modeling (He et al., 2021). Then we proposed a new method which consists on keeping in cache the previous retrieval distributions so that the model does not need to search for neighbors in the datastore at every step. Through experiments on domain adaptation, we show that the combination of the proposed methods leads to a considerable speed-up (up to 2x) without harming the translation performance substantially.

Acknowledgments

This work was supported by the European Research Council (ERC StG DeepSPIN 758969), by the P2020 project MAIA (contract 045909), by the Fundação para a Ciência e Tecnologia through project PTDC/CCI-INF/4703/2021 (PRELUNA, contract UIDB/50008/2020), and by contract PD/BD/150633/2020 in the scope of the Doctoral Program FCT - PD/00140/2013 NETSyS. We thank Junxian He, Graham Neubig, the SARDINE team members, and the reviewers for helpful discussion and feedback.

References

Roee Aharoni and Yoav Goldberg. 2020. Unsupervised domain clusters in pretrained language models. In *Proc. ACL*.

Dzmitry Bahdanau, Kyung Hyun Cho, and Yoshua Bengio. 2015. Neural machine translation by jointly learning to align and translate. In *Proc. ICLR*.

Ankur Bapna and Orhan Firat. 2019. Non-Parametric Adaptation for Neural Machine Translation. In *Proc. NAACL*.

Jiatao Gu, Yong Wang, Kyunghyun Cho, and Victor OK Li. 2018. Search engine guided neural machine translation. In *Proc. AAAI*.

Junxian He, Graham Neubig, and Taylor Berg-Kirkpatrick. 2021. Efficient Nearest Neighbor Language Models. In *Proc. EMNLP*.

Qingnan Jiang, Mingxuan Wang, Jun Cao, Shanbo Cheng, Shujian Huang, and Lei Li. 2021. Learning Kernel-Smoothed Machine Translation with Retrieved Examples. In *Proc. EMNLP*.

Jeff Johnson, Matthijs Douze, and Hervé Jégou. 2019. Billion-scale similarity search with gpus. *IEEE Transactions on Big Data*.

Urvashi Khandelwal, Angela Fan, Dan Jurafsky, Luke Zettlemoyer, and Mike Lewis. 2021. Nearest neighbor machine translation. In *Proc. ICLR*.

Philipp Koehn and Rebecca Knowles. 2017. Six Challenges for Neural Machine Translation. In *Proceedings of the First Workshop on Neural Machine Translation*.

Yuxian Meng, Xiaoya Li, Xiayu Zheng, Fei Wu, Xiaofei Sun, Tianwei Zhang, and Jiwei Li. 2021. Fast Nearest Neighbor Machine Translation.

Nathan Ng, Kyra Yee, Alexei Baevski, Myle Ott, Michael Auli, and Sergey Edunov. 2019. Facebook FAIR's WMT19 News Translation Task Submission. In *Proc. of the Fourth Conference on Machine Translation*.

Myle Ott, Sergey Edunov, Alexei Baevski, Angela Fan, Sam Gross, Nathan Ng, David Grangier, and Michael Auli. 2019. fairseq: A Fast, Extensible Toolkit for Sequence Modeling. In *Proc. NAACL (Demonstrations)*.

Kishore Papineni, Salim Roukos, Todd Ward, and Wei-Jing Zhu. 2002. Bleu: a method for automatic evaluation of machine translation. In *Proc. ACL*.

Matt Post. 2018. A Call for Clarity in Reporting BLEU Scores. In *Proc. Third Conference on Machine Translation*.

Ricardo Rei, Craig Stewart, Ana C Farinha, and Alon Lavie. 2020. COMET: A Neural Framework for MT Evaluation. In *Proc. EMNLP*.

Danielle Saunders. 2021. Domain Adaptation and Multi-Domain Adaptation for Neural Machine Translation: A Survey.

Ashish Vaswani, Noam Shazeer, Niki Parmar, Jakob Uszkoreit, Llion Jones, Aidan N Gomez, Łukasz Kaiser, and Illia Polosukhin. 2017. Attention is all you need. In *Proc. NeurIPS*.

Jingyi Zhang, Masao Utiyama, Eiichiro Sumita, Graham Neubig, and Satoshi Nakamura. 2018. Guiding Neural Machine Translation with Retrieved Translation Pieces. In *Proc. NAACL*.

Xin Zheng, Zhirui Zhang, Junliang Guo, Shujian Huang, Boxing Chen, Weihua Luo, and Jiajun Chen. 2021. Adaptive Nearest Neighbor Machine Translation.

A Additional results

In this section we report the BLEU scores as well as additional statistics for the different methods, when varying their hyper-parameters.

A.1 Datastore pruning

We report on Table 2 the BLEU scores for datastore pruning, when varying the number of neighbors used for greedy merging, k. The resulting datastore sizes are presented on Table 3.

	Medical	Law	IT	Koran	Average
kNN-MT	54.47	61.23	45.96	21.02	45.67
$k=1$	53.60	60.23	45.03	20.81	44.92
$k=2$	52.95	59.40	44.76	20.12	44.31
$k=5$	51.63	57.55	44.07	19.29	43.14

Table 2: BLEU scores on the multi-domains test set when performing datastore pruning with several values of k, for a batch size of 8.

	Medical	Law	IT	Koran
kNN-MT	6,903,141	19,061,382	3,602,862	524,374
$k=1$	4,780,514	13,130,326	2,641,709	400,385
$k=2$	4,039,432	11,103,775	2,303,808	353,007
$k=5$	3,084,106	8,486,551	1,852,191	290,192

Table 3: Sizes of the in-domain datastores when performing datastore pruning with several values of k, for a batch size of 8.

A.2 Dimension reduction

We report on Table 4 the BLEU scores for dimension reduction, when varying the output dimension d.

	Medical	Law	IT	Koran	Average
kNN-MT	54.47	61.23	45.96	21.02	45.67
$d=512$	55.06	62.04	46.98	21.24	46.33
$d=256$	54.52	61.84	46.68	21.57	46.15
$d=128$	53.94	61.17	45.46	21.35	45.48

Table 4: BLEU scores on the multi-domains test set when performing PCA with different dimension, d, values, for a batch size of 8.

A.3 Adaptive retrieval

We report on Table 5 the BLEU scores for adaptive retrieval, when varying the threshold α. The percentage of times the model performs retrieval is stated on Table 6.

	Medical	Law	IT	Koran	Average
kNN-MT	54.47	61.23	45.96	21.02	45.67
$\alpha=0.25$	45.52	49.91	37.97	16.36	37.44
$\alpha=0.5$	52.84	59.36	38.58	18.08	42.22
$\alpha=0.75$	53.90	60.87	43.05	19.91	44.43

Table 5: BLEU scores on the multi-domains test set when performing adaptive retrieval for different values of the threshold α, for a batch size of 8.

	Medical	Law	IT	Koran
kNN-MT	100%	100%	100%	100%
$\alpha=0.25$	78%	73%	38%	4%
$\alpha=0.5$	96%	96%	60%	61%
$\alpha=0.75$	98%	99%	92%	91%

Table 6: Percentage of times the model searches for neighbors on the datastore when performing adaptive retrieval for different values of the threshold α, for a batch size of 8.

A.4 Cache

We report on Table 7 the BLEU scores for a model using a cache of the retrieval distributions, when varying the threshold τ. The percentage of times the model performs retrieval is stated on Table 8.

	Medical	Law	IT	Koran	Average
kNN-MT	54.47	61.23	45.96	21.02	45.67
$\tau=2$	54.47	61.23	45.93	20.98	45.65
$\tau=4$	54.17	61.10	46.07	21.00	45.58
$\tau=6$	53.30	59.12	45.39	20.67	44.62
$\tau=8$	30.06	23.01	25.53	16.08	23.67

Table 7: BLEU scores on the multi-domains test set when using a retrieval distributions' cache for different values of the threshold τ, for a batch size of 8.

	Medical	Law	IT	Koran
kNN-MT	100%	100%	100%	100%
$\tau=2$	59%	51%	67%	64%
$\tau=4$	50%	42%	57%	53%
$\tau=6$	43%	35%	49%	45%
$\tau=8$	26%	16%	29%	31%

Table 8: Percentage of times the model searches for neighbors on the datastore when using a retrieval distributions' cache for different values of the threshold τ, for a batch size of 8.

B Hyper-parameters

On Table 9 we report the values for the hyper-parameters: number of neighbors to be retrieved

	Medical			Law			IT			Koran		
	k	λ	T	k	λ	T	k	λ	T	k	λ	T
kNN-MT	8	0.7	10	8	0.8	10	8	0.7	10	8	0.6	100
Fast kNN-MT	16	0.7	.015	32	0.6	.015	8	0.6	.02	16	0.6	.05
cache	8	0.7	10	8	0.8	10	8	0.7	10	8	0.6	100
PCA + cache	8	0.8	10	8	0.8	10	8	0.7	10	8	0.7	100
PCA + pruning	8	0.7	10	8	0.8	10	8	0.7	10	8	0.7	100
PCA + cache + pruning	8	0.7	10	8	0.8	10	8	0.7	10	8	0.7	100

Table 9: Values of the hyper-parameters: number of neighbors to be retrieved k, interpolation coefficient λ, and retrieval softmax temperature T.

$k \in \{8, 16, 32, 64\}$, the interpolation coefficient $\lambda \in \{0.5, 0.6, 0.7, 0.8\}$, and retrieval softmax temperature T. For decoding we use beam search with a beam size of 5.

Field Extraction from Forms with Unlabeled Data

Mingfei Gao, Zeyuan Chen, Nikhil Naik, Kazuma Hashimoto, Caiming Xiong, Ran Xu
Salesforce Research, Palo Alto, USA
{mingfei.gao, zeyuan.chen, nnaik, k.hashimoto, cxiong, ran.xu}@salesforce.com

Abstract

We propose a novel framework to conduct field extraction from forms with unlabeled data. To bootstrap the training process, we develop a rule-based method for mining noisy pseudo-labels from unlabeled forms. Using the supervisory signal from the pseudo-labels, we extract a discriminative token representation from a transformer-based model by modeling the interaction between text in the form. To prevent the model from overfitting to label noise, we introduce a refinement module based on a progressive pseudo-label ensemble. Experimental results demonstrate the effectiveness of our framework.

Field (purchase_order): [PO Number, PO #]

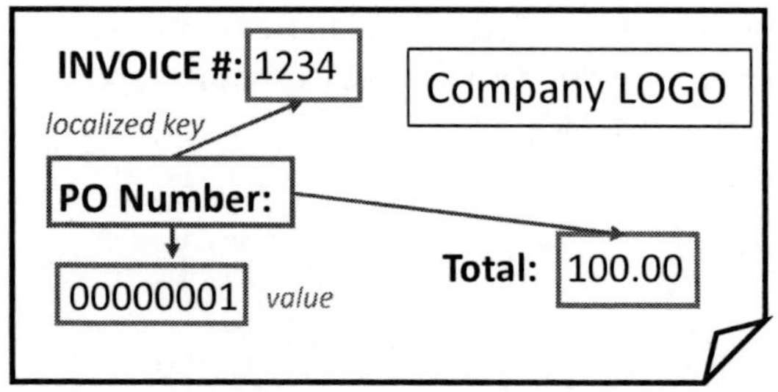

Figure 1: Field extraction from forms is to extract the value for each field, e.g., *invoice_number*, *purchase_order* and *total_amount*, in a given list. A key, e.g., INVOICE#, PO Number and Total, refers to a concrete text representation of a field in a form and it is an important indicator for value localization.

1 Introduction

Form-like documents, such as invoices, paystubs and patient referral forms, are very common in daily business workflows. A large amount of human effort is required to extract information from forms every day. In form processing, a worker is usually given a list of expected form fields (e.g., *purchase_order*, *invoice_number* and *total_amount* in Figure 1), and the goal is to extract their corresponding values based on the understanding of the form, where keys are generally the most important features for value localization. A field extraction system aims to automatically extract field values from redundant information in forms, which is crucial for improving processing efficiency and reducing human labor.

Field extraction from forms is a challenging task. Document layouts and text representations can be very different even for the same form type, if they are from different vendors. For example, invoices from different companies may have significantly different designs (see Figure 3). Paystubs from different systems (e.g., ADP and Workday) have different representations for similar information.

Recent methods formulate this problem as field-value pairing or field tagging. Majumder et al. (2020) propose a representation learning method that takes field and value candidates as inputs and utilizes metric learning techniques to enforce high pairing score for positive field-value pairs and low score for negative ones. LayoutLM (Xu et al., 2020) is a pretrained transformer that takes both text and their locations as inputs. It can be used as a field-tagger which predicts field tags for input texts. These methods show promising results, but they require large amount of field-level annotations for training. Acquiring field-level annotations of forms is challenging and sometimes even impossible since (1) forms usually contain sensitive information, so there is limited public data available; (2) working with external annotators is also infeasible, due to the risk of exposing private information and (3) annotating field-level labels is time-consuming and hard to scale.

Motivated by these reasons, we propose a field extraction system that does not require field-level annotations for training (see Figure 2). First, we bootstrap the training process by mining pseudo-labels from unlabeled forms using simple rules. Then, a transformer-based architecture is used to

Proceedings of the 1st Workshop on Semiparametric Methods in NLP: Decoupling Logic from Knowledge, pages 30 - 40
May 27, 2022 ©2022 Association for Computational Linguistics

model interactions between text tokens in the form and predict a field tag for each token accordingly. The pseudo-labels are used to supervise the transformer training. Since the pseudo-labels are noisy, we propose a refinement module to improve the learning process. Specifically, the refinement module contains a sequence of branches, each of which conducts field tagging and generates refined labels. At each stage, a branch is optimized by the labels ensembled from all previous branches to reduce label noise. Our method shows strong performance on real invoice datasets. Each designed module is validated via comprehensive ablation experiments.

Our contribution is summarized as follows: (1) to the best of our knowledge, this is the first work that addresses the problem of field extraction from forms without using field-level labels; (2) we propose a novel training framework where simple rules are first used to bootstrap the training process and a transformer-based model is used to improve performance; (3) our proposed refinement module is demonstrated as effective to improve model performance when trained with noisy labels and (4) to facilitate future research, we introduce the INV-CDIP dataset as a public benchmark. The dataset is available at https://github.com/salesforce/inv-cdip.

2 Related Work

2.1 Form understanding

Form understanding is a widely researched area. Earlier work formulated the problem as an instance segmentation task. Chargrid (Katti et al., 2018) encodes each page of form as a two-dimensional grid of characters, and extracts header and line items from forms using fully convolutional networks. Based on Chargrid, Denk and Reisswig (2019) propose BERTgrid which uses a grid of contextualized word embedding vectors to represent documents. These methods are limited in scenarios where the image resolution is not high enough leading to sub-optimal representation of ambiguous structures in dense regions. To mitigate the issue, later methods work on structure modeling. Aggarwal et al. (2020) introduce Form2Seq to leverage relative spatial arrangement of structures via first conducting low-level element classification and then high-order grouping. DocStruct (Wang et al., 2020) encodes the form structure as a graph-like hierarchy of text fragments and designs a hybrid fusion method to provide joint representation from multiple modalities. Benefiting from the recent advances of transformers (Vaswani et al., 2017), LayoutLM (Xu et al., 2020) learns text representation via modeling the interaction between text tokens and their locations in documents.

There are dedicated methods focusing on field extraction. Some methods (Chiticariu et al., 2013; Schuster et al., 2013) extract information from document via registering templates in the system. Palm et al. (2019) propose an Attend, Copy, Parse architecture to extract field values of invoices. Majumder et al. (2020) present a metric learning framework that learns the representation of the value candidate based on its nearby words and matches the field-value pairs using a learned scoring function. Gao et al. (2021) propose a general value extraction system for arbitrary queries and introduce a simple pretraining strategy to improve document understanding. Although existing approaches demonstrate promising results in different settings, they rely on large-scale annotated data for training. For example, Majumder et al. (2020) used more than 11,000 invoices in distinct templates for training.

2.2 Form datasets

Form datasets for field extraction tasks are typically private, since these documents generally contain sensitive information. There are existing public datasets for general form understanding. RVL-CDIP (Harley et al., 2015) and DocVQA (Mathew et al., 2021) are introduced for document classification and question answering tasks. FUNSD (Jaume et al., 2019) dataset is organized as a list of interlinked semantic entities, i.e., question, answer, header and other. CORD (Park et al., 2019) is a public receipt dataset focusing on line items. SROIE (Huang et al., 2019) is the most related dataset which aims to extract information for four receipt-related fields. However, their layouts across different receipts are very fixed, which makes it less challenging, thus not suitable for our task. For example, the values of fields, *company* and *address*, are always on the very top in all the receipts. The lack of appropriate public datasets makes it difficult to compare existing field extraction methods on realistic forms. Xue et al. (2021) introduce a framework to augment diverse forms from a small set of annotated forms for robust evaluation. In this work, we introduce a challenging and real invoice dataset that is made publicly available to future research.

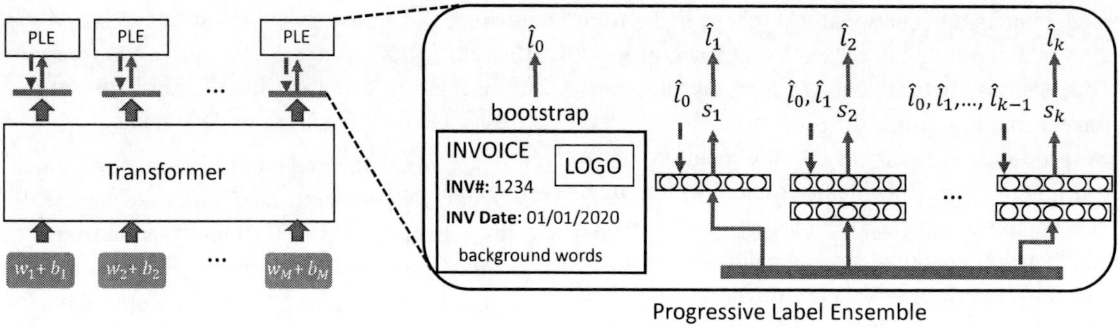

Figure 2: Our method takes words, w_i, and their locations, b_i, in a form into a transformer. The transformer extracts representative features for each token via the self-attention mechanism. Since our method is trained using forms with no field labels, we design progressive label ensemble module to enable the training process. We bootstrap the initial pseudo-labels, $\hat{l}_0$, using simple rules. Then, token representations go through several branches and do the field prediction as well as label refinement. Each branch, j, is optimized with labels ensembled from all previous branches, $\hat{l}_0, \hat{l}_1, ..., \hat{l}_{j-1}$.

3 Field Extraction from Forms

3.1 Problem Formulation

We are interested in information of fields in a predefined list, $\{fd_1, fd_2, ..., fd_N\}$. Given a form as input, a general OCR detection and recognition module is applied to obtain a set of words, $\{w_1, w_2, ..., w_M\}$, with their locations represented as bounding boxes, $\{b_1, b_2, ..., b_M\}$. The goal of a field extraction method is to automatically extract the target value, v_i, of field, fd_i, from the massive word candidates if the information of the field exists in the input form.

Unlike previous methods that have access to large-scale labeled forms, the proposed method can be trained using unlabeled documents with known form types. To achieve this goal, we propose a simple rule-based method to mine noisy pseudo-labels from unlabeled data (Sec. 3.2) and introduce a data-driven method with a refinement module to improve training with noisy labels (Sec. 3.3).

3.2 Bootstrap: Pseudo-Labels Inference from Unlabeled Data

To bootstrap the training process, given unlabeled forms, we first mine pseudo-labels using a simple rule-based algorithm. The algorithm is motivated by the following observations: (1) a field value usually shows together with some key and the key is a concrete text representation of the field (see Figure 1); (2) the keys and their corresponding values have strong geometric relations. As shown in Figure 1, the keys are mostly next to their values vertically or horizontally; (3) although the form's layout is very diverse, there are usually some key-texts that frequently used in different form instances. For example, the key-texts of the field *purchase_order* can be "PO Number", "PO #" etc. and (4) inspired by Majumder et al. (2020), the field values are always associated with some data type. For example, the data type of values of "invoice_date" is *date* and that of "total_amount" is *money* or *number*.

Based on the above observations, we design a simple rule-based method that can efficiently get useful pseudo-labels for each field of interest from large-scale forms. As shown in Figure 1, key localization is first conducted based on string-matching between text in a form and possible key strings of a field. Then, values are estimated based on data types of the text and their geometric relationship with the localized key.

Key Localization. Since keys and values may contain multiple words, we obtain phrase candidates, $[ph_i^1, ph_i^2, ..., ph_i^T]$, and their locations $[B_i^1, B_i^2, ..., B_i^T]$ in the form by grouping nearby recognized words based on their locations using DBSCAN algorithm (Ester et al., 1996). For each field of interest, fd_i, we design a list of frequently used keys, $[k_i^1, k_i^2, ..., k_i^L]$, based on domain knowledge. In practice, we can also use the field name as the only key in the list. Then, we measure the string distance[1] between a phrase candidate, ph_i^j, and each designed key, k_i^r, as $d(ph_i^j, k_i^r)$. We calculate the key score for each phrase candidate indicating how likely this candidate is to be a key for the field using Eq. 1. Finally, the key is localized

[1] Without loss of generality, Jaro–Winkler distance (Winkler, 1990) is used in this work.

by finding the candidate with the largest key score as in Eq. 2.

$$key\_score(ph_i^j) = 1 - \min_{r \in \{1,2,...,L\}} d(ph_i^j, k_i^r). \tag{1}$$

$$\hat{k}_i = \underset{j \in \{1,2,...,T\}}{argmax}\ key\_score(ph_i^j). \tag{2}$$

Value Estimation. Values are estimated following two criteria. First, their data type should be in line with their fields. Second, their locations should accord well with the localized keys. For each field, we design a list of eligible data type (see Table A1 in the appendix, Sec. A). A pretrained BERT-based NER model (Devlin et al., 2019) is used to predict the data type of each phrase candidate and we only keep the candidates, ph_i^j, with the correct data type.

Next, we assign a value score for each eligible candidate, ph_i^j as in Eq. 3, where $key\_score(\hat{k}_i)$ indicates the key score of the localized key and $g(ph_i^j, \hat{k}_i)$ denotes the geometric relation score between the candidate and the localized key. Intuitively, the key and its value are generally close to each other and the values are likely to just beneath the key or reside on their right side as shown in Figure 1. So, we use distance and angles to measure key-value relation as shown in Eq. 4, where $dist_i^{j \to r}$ indicates the distance of two phrases, $angle_i^{j \to r}$ indicates the angle from ph_i^j to ph_i^r and $\Phi(.|\mu, \sigma)$ indicates Gaussian function with μ as mean and σ as standard deviation. Here, we set μ_d to 0. σ_d and σ_a are fixed to 0.5. We want to reward the candidates whose angle with respect to the key is close either to 0 or $\pi/2$, so we take the maximum angle score of these two options.

$$value\_score(ph_i^j) = key\_score(\hat{k}_i) * g(\hat{k}_i, ph_i^j). \tag{3}$$

$$g(ph_i^j, ph_i^r) = \Phi(dist_i^{j \to r}|\mu_d, \sigma_d) + \alpha \max_{\mu_a \in \{0, \pi/2\}} \Phi(angle_i^{j \to r}|\mu_a, \sigma_a). \tag{4}$$

$$\hat{v}_i = \underset{j \in \{1,2,...,T\}, ph_i^j \neq \hat{k}_i}{argmax} value\_score(ph_i^j). \tag{5}$$

We determine a candidate as the predicted value for a field if its value score is the largest among all candidates as in Eq. 5 and the score exceeds a threshold, $\theta_v = 0.1$.

3.3 Refinement with Progressive Pseudo-Labels Ensemble (PLE)

The above rule can be used directly as a simple field extraction method. To further improve performance, we can learn a data-driven model using the estimated values of fields as pseudo-labels during training. We formulate this as a token classification task, where the input is a set of tokens extracted from a form and the output is the predicted field including background for each token.

Feature Backbone. To predict the target label of a word, we need to understand the meaning of this word as well as its interaction with the surrounding context. Transformer-based architecture is a good fit to learn the word's representation for its great capability of modeling contextual information. Except for the semantic representation, the word's location and the general layout of the input form are also important and could be used to capture discriminative features of words. In practice, we used the recently proposed LayoutLM (Xu et al., 2020) as the default backbone and also experimented with other transformer-based structures in Sec. 4.

Field Classification. Field prediction scores, s_k, are obtained by projecting the features to the field space ($\{background, fd_1, fd_2, ..., fd_N\}$) via fully connected (FC) layers.

Progressive Pseudo-Labels Ensemble. Initial word-level field labels (also referred to as Bootstrap Labels), $\hat{l}_0$, are obtained by the estimated pseudo-labels from Sec. 3.2 and the network can be optimized using cross entropy loss, $L(s_k, \hat{l}_0)$. However, naively using the noisy labels can degrade the model performance. We introduce a refinement module to tackle this issue. As shown in Figure 2, we use a sequence of classification branches, where each branch, j, conducts field classification independently and refines pseudo-labels, $\hat{l}_j$, based on their predictions. A later-stage branch is optimized using the refined labels obtained from previous branches. The final loss, L_{total}, aggregates all the losses as

$$L(s_1, \hat{l}_0) + \sum_{k=2}^{K} \sum_{j=1}^{k-1} (L(s_k, \hat{l}_j) + \beta L(s_k, \hat{l}_0)), \tag{6}$$

where β is a hyper parameter controlling the contribution of the initial pseudo-labels.

At branch k, we generate refined labels according to the following steps: (1) find the predicted field label, $\hat{fd}$, for each word by $\underset{c \in \{0,1,...,N\}}{argmax}\ s_{kc}$ and

(2) for each positive field, only keep the word if its prediction score is the highest among all the words and larger than a threshold (fixed to 0.1).

Intuitively, each branch can be improved by using more accurate labels and its generated labels are further refined. This progressive refinement of labels reduces label noise. Similar idea has been used in weakly supervised object detection (Tang et al., 2017). However, we find that using only the refined labels in each stage is limited in our setting, because although the labels become more precise after refinement, some low-confident values are filtered out which results in lower recall. To alleviate this issue, we optimize a branch with the ensembled labels from all previous stages. We believe that the ensembeled labels can not only keep a better balance between precision and recall, but also are more diverse and can serve as a regularization for model optimization. During inference, we use the average score predicted from all branches. We follow the same procedure to get final field values as we generate refine labels.

4 Experiments and Results

4.1 Datasets

IN-Invoice Dataset. We internally collect real invoices from different vendors. These invoice images are converted from real PDFs, so they are in high resolution with clean background. The train set contains 7,664 **unlabeled** invoice forms of 2,711 vendors. The validation set contains 348 **labeled** invoices of 222 vendors. The test set contains 339 **labeled** invoices of 222 vendors. We manually ensure that at most 5 images are from the same vendor in each set. Following Majumder et al. (2020), we consider 7 frequently used fields including *invoice_number*, *purchase_order*, *invoice_date*, *due_date*, *amount_due*, *total_amount* and *total_tax*.

INV-CDIP. This dataset is from the Tobacco Collections of Industry Documents Library [2], a publicly accessible resource. The dataset contains 200k noisy documents. We only keep the first page of each document, since the invoice information is most likely to show in page one. To reduce the number of noisy samples, we only train on documents if they have 50-300 words (detected by our OCR engine) and more than 3 invoice fields are found by our rule-based method in Sec. 3.2. As a result, we have 129k unlabeled training samples.

For model evaluation, we manually select 350 real invoices as the test set and annotate the 7 fields mentioned above. We note that images of this dataset have lower quality and more clutter background (see Figure 3) which make them more challenging than the IN-Invoice dataset.

More information of the datasets is illustrated in the appendix (Sec. A).

4.2 Evaluation Metric

We use the macro-average of end-to-end F1 score over fields as a metric to evaluate models. Specifically, exact string matching between our predicted values and the ground-truth ones is used to count true positive, false positive and false negative. Precision, recall and F1 score is obtained accordingly for each field. The reported scores are averaged over 5 runs to reduce the effect of randomness.

4.3 Baselines

It is challenging to compare our method with existing field extraction systems, since they have been evaluated using different datasets in different settings. To the best of our knowledge, there are no existing methods that perform field extraction using only unlabeled data. So, we build the following baselines to validate our method.

Bootstrap Labels (B-Labels): the proposed simple rules in Sec. 3.2 can be used to do field extraction directly without training data. So, we first show the effectiveness of this method and set up a baseline for later comparison.

Transformers train with B-Labels: since we use transformers as the backbone to extract features of words, we train transformer models using the B-Labels as baselines to evaluate the performance gain from (1) the data-driven models in the pipeline and (2) the refinement module. Both the content of the text and its location are important for field prediction. So, our default transformer backbone is LayoutLM (Xu et al., 2020) which takes both text and location as input. Further, we also experiment with two popular transformer models, i.e., BERT (Devlin et al., 2019) and RoBERTa (Liu et al., 2019), which take only text as input.

4.4 Implementation Details

. Our framework is implemented using Pytorch and the experiments are conducted with Tesla V100 GPUs. We use a commercial OCR engine[3] to de-

[2]https://www.industrydocuments.ucsf.edu/.

[3]https://api.einstein.ai/signup

tect words and their locations and use Tesseract[4] to rank the words in reading order. The key list and data type used in Sec. 3.2 for each dataset are shown in Table A1 in Sec. A. As we can see, the key lists and data types are quite broad. We set α in Eq. 4 to 4.0. To further remove false positives, we remove the value candidates if the localized key is not within its neighboring zone. Specifically, we define the neighboring zone around the value candidate extending all the way to the left of the image, four candidate heights above it and one candidate height below it. We keep the refine branch number $k = 3$ for all experiments. We add one hidden FC layer with 768 units before classification when stage number is > 1. We fix β in Eq. 6 to be 1.0 for all invoice experiments, except that we use $\beta = 5.0$ for BERT-base refinement in Table 3 due to its better performance in the validation set. For both our model and baselines, we train models for 2 epochs and pick the model with the best F1 score in validation set. To prevent overfitting, we adopt a two-step training strategy, where the pseudo-labels are used to train the first branch of our model and then we fix the first branch along with the feature extractor during the refinement. We set batch size to 8 and use the Adam optimizer with learning rate of $5e^{-5}$.

4.5 Comparison with Baselines

Main Comparison. We primarily validate our design using our IN-Invoice dateset, since it contains large-scale clean, unlabeled training data and sufficient amount of valid/test data. We first validate our method using LayoutLM (our default choice) as the backbone. The comparison results are shown in Table 1 and Table 2. The Bootstrap Labels (B-Labels) baseline achieves 43.8% and 44.1% F1 score in valid and test sets, which indicates that our B-Labels have reasonable accuracy, but are still noisy. When we use the B-Labels to train a LayoutLM transformer, we obtain a significant performance improvement, $\sim$15% increase in valid set and $\sim$17% in test set. We tried both LayoutLM-base (113M parameters) and LayoutLM-large (343M parameters) models as backbones and we did not see performance improvement when using a larger model. Adding our refinement module significantly improves model precision, $\sim$6% in valid set and $\sim$7% in test set, while slightly decreasing the recall, $\sim$2.5% in valid set and $\sim$3% in test set. This is because the refine labels become more and more confident in later stages leading to higher model precision. However, the refinement stage also removes some low confidence false negatives which results in lower recall. Overall, our refinement module further improves performance, resulting in a gain of $\sim$ 3% in F1 score.

Results with Different Transformers. We use LayoutLM as the default feature backbone, since both the text and its location is important for our task. To understand the impact of different transformer models as backbone, we experiment with two additional models, BERT and RoBERTa, where only text is used as input. The comparison results are shown in Table 3 and Table 4. We have the following observations: (1) we still obtain large improvement when training BERT and RoBERTa directly using our B-Labels and (2) our refinement module consistently improves the baseline results for different transformer choices with different amount of parameters (base or large). Moreover, LayoutLM yields much higher results compared to the other two backbones, which indicates that the text location is indeed very important for obtaining good performance in our task.

Evaluation on INV-CDIP Test Set. We evaluate our models trained using IN-Invoice data directly on the introduced INV-CDIP test set in Table 5. Our simple rule-based method obtains 25.1% F1 score which is reasonable, but much lower compared to the results on our internal IN-Invoice dataset. The reason is that the INV-CDIP test set is visually noisy which results in more OCR recognition errors. The LayoutLM baselines still obtain large improvements over the B-Labels baseline. Also, our refinement module further improves more than 2% in F1 score. The results suggest that our method adapts well to the new dataset. We show some visualizations in Figure 3. We can see that our method obtains good performance, although the invoices are very diverse across different templates, have cluttered background and are in low resolution.

Learning from Noisy INV-CDIP Data. Although web data is noisy, it can be freely obtained from the internet. We train our model and the baseline model using the unlabeled train set of the noisy INV-CDIP dataset. The comparison results are shown in Table 6 (all models are base models). As we can see, our method performs well and our PLE module can still improves the baseline by about 2-3%, although the training set is very noisy.

[4] https://github.com/tesseract-ocr/tesseract

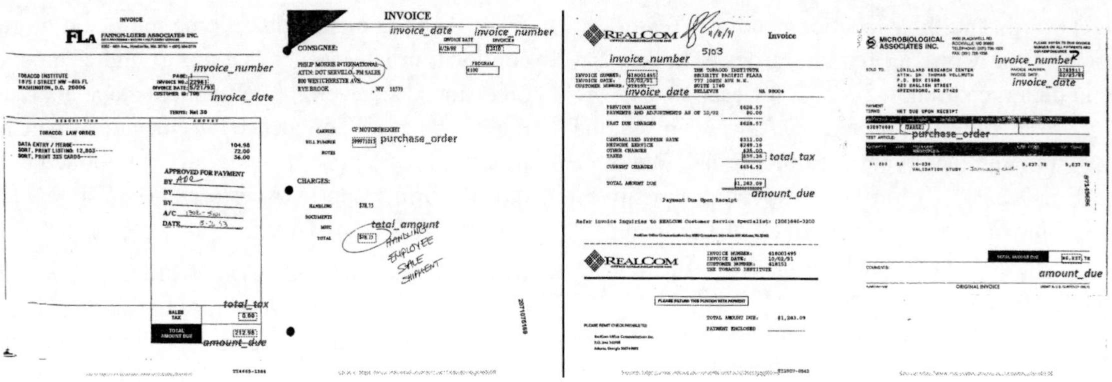

Figure 3: Visualization of our method on the INV-CDIP test set. Correct predictions are marked in red font. Incorrect predictions are marked in blue (due to field extractor error) and purple (due to OCR recognition error).

Model	Labels	Prec.	Rec.	F1
Bootstrap Labels	–	40.5	50.7	43.8
LayoutLM-base	B-Labels	54.8	66.6	59.2
+ **PLE**		60.9	64.0	**61.9**
LayoutLM-large		55.2	65.6	58.8
+ **PLE**		61.3	63.2	**61.8**

Table 1: Comparison with baselines on IN-Invoice valid set. Models are trained using the unlabeled IN-Invoice train set.

Model	Labels	Prec.	Rec.	F1
Bootstrap Labels	–	41.0	50.9	44.1
LayoutLM-base	B-Labels	57.5	67.6	61.2
+ **PLE**		64.7	64.5	**63.8**
LayoutLM-large		58.2	67.1	61.0
+ **PLE**		65.6	64.0	**64.1**

Table 2: Comparison with baselines on IN-Invoice test set. Models are trained using the unlabeled IN-Invoice train set.

4.6 Ablation Study

We conduct ablation study on the IN-Invoice dataset with LayoutLM-base as the backbone.

Effect of Stage Numbers. Our model is refined in k stages, where $k = 3$ in all experiments. We evaluate our method with varying stage numbers. As we can see in Figure 4, when we increase the stage number, k, the model generally performs better on both valid and test sets. The performance with more than one stage is always higher than the single-stage model (our transformer baseline). Model performance reaches the highest when $k = 3$. As shown in Figure 5, precision improves while recall drops during model refinement. When $k = 3$, we obtain the best balance between precision and recall. When $k > 3$ recall drops more than precision improves, leading to a lower F1 score.

Effect of Refined Labels (R-Labels). As shown in Figure 2, the R-Labels obtained in each stage are used in later stages. To analyze the effect of this design, we remove the refined labels in the

Model	Labels	Prec.	Rec.	F1
Bootstrap Labels	–	40.5	50.7	43.8
BERT-base	B-Labels	48.8	59.6	52.8
+ **PLE**		49.9	59.3	**53.4**
BERT-large		53.7	60.9	56.5
+ **PLE**		58.0	59.4	**58.1**
RoBERTa-base		55.1	60.5	57.2
+ **PLE**		59.9	58.0	**58.5**
RoBERTa-large		55.3	61.8	57.8
+ **PLE**		60.5	60.1	**59.1**

Table 3: Comparison using different transformers on IN-Invoice valid set. Models are trained using the unlabeled IN-Invoice train set.

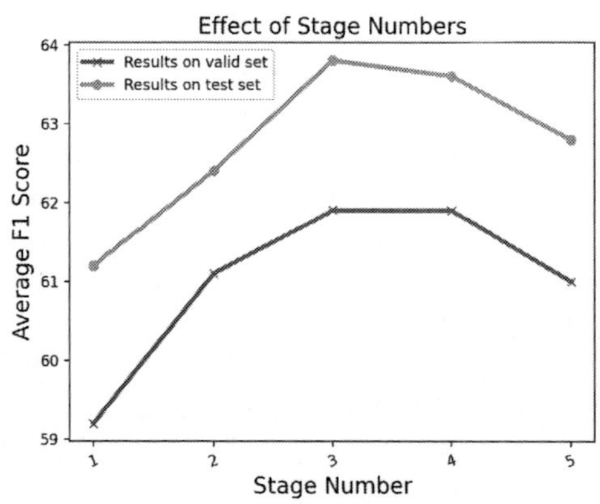

Figure 4: Comparison results with varying stage numbers. When stage number is 1, the model becomes the LayoutLM baseline.

Model	Labels	Prec.	Rec.	F1
Bootstrap Labels	–	41.0	50.9	44.1
BERT-base	B-Labels	51.3	61.4	54.9
+ PLE		52.6	61.0	**55.6**
BERT-large		55.7	61.7	57.7
+ PLE		60.2	58.8	**58.6**
RoBERTa-base		57.2	61.4	58.7
+ PLE		62.7	58.6	**59.8**
RoBERTa-large		56.3	61.4	57.8
+ PLE		62.5	59.6	**59.2**

Table 4: Comparison using different transformers on IN-Invoice test set. Models are trained using the unlabeled IN-Invoice train set.

Model	Labels	Prec.	Rec.	F1
Bootstrap Labels	–	21.8	36	25.1
LayoutLM-base	B-Labels	31.6	44.6	35.2
+ PLE		37.3	40.9	**37.3**
LayoutLM-large		33.8	46.5	36.9
+ PLE		40.2	42.2	**39.4**

Table 5: Comparison with baselines on INV-CDIP test set. Models are trained using the unlabeled IN-Invoice train set.

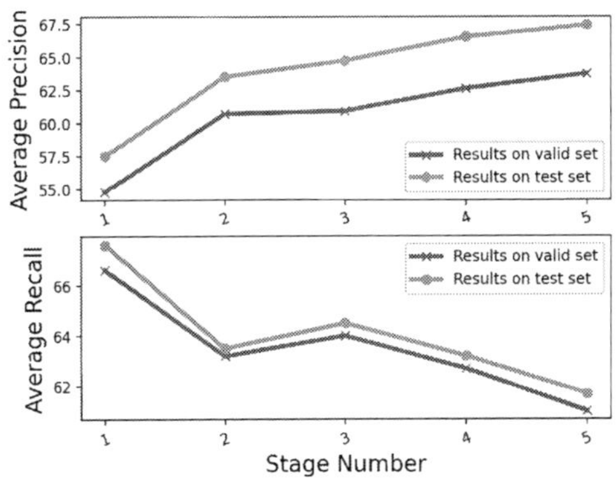

Figure 5: In general, our model has higher precision, but lower recall with larger number of branches.

final loss and only use the B-Labels to train the three branches independently and ensemble the predictions during inference. As shown in Table 7, removing refined labels results in 2.2% and 2.6% decrease in F1 scores in valid and test sets.

Effect of Regularization with B-Labels. At each stage, we use B-Labels as a type of regularization to prevent the model from overfitting to the over-confident refined labels. We disable the utilization of B-Labels in the refinement stage by setting $\beta = 0$ in Eq. 6. As we can see in Table 7, model

Model	Eval Set	Prec.	Rec.	F1
LayoutLM	IN-Inv Val	46.3	60.6	51.4
+ PLE		51.7	58.6	**54.2**
LayoutLM	IN-Inv Test	47.8	62.3	52.9
+ PLE		53.0	59.2	**55.1**
LayoutLM	INV-CDIP Test	28.0	47.5	32.8
+ PLE		31.0	46.4	**35.4**

Table 6: Comparison with baselines when methods are trained using the noisy INV-CDIP train set.

Set	R-Labels	2-step train	B-Labels	F1
Valid		√	√	59.7
	√		√	60.1
	√	√		60.0
	√	√	√	**61.9**
Test		√	√	61.2
	√		√	62.4
	√	√		61.6
	√	√	√	**63.8**

Table 7: Results of ablation study.

performance drops $\sim$2% in F1 score without this regularization.

Effect of Two-step Training Strategy. To avoid overfitting to noisy labels, we adopt two-step training strategy, where the transformer backbone with the first branch is trained using B-Labels and then fixed during the refinement. We analyze this effect by training our model in a single step. As shown in Table 7, single-step training leads to 1.8% and 1.4% F1 score decrease in valid and test sets.

4.7 Limitations and Future Work

Our work focuses on training models using unlabeled forms. An interesting future avenue would be to utilize additional labeled data in a semi-supervised setting. Moreover, validating our methods with more form types would also be valuable. We will consider these topics in future work.

5 Conclusion

We proposed a field extraction system that can be trained using forms without field-level annotations. We first introduced a rule-based method to get initial pseudo-labels of forms. Then, we proposed a transformer-based method and improved the model using progressively ensembled labels. We demonstrated that our method outperforms the baselines on invoice datasets and each component of our method makes considerable contribution.

6 Broader Impact

This work is potentially useful for improving information extraction systems from forms. So, it has positive impacts including improving document processing efficiency, thus reducing human labor. Reducing human labor may also cause negative consequences such as job loss or displacement, particularly amongst low-skilled labor who may be most in need of gainful employment. The negative impact is not specific to this work and should be addressed broadly in the field of AI research.

We are securely using the IN-Invoice dataset internally. For the public data in the INV-CDIP dataset, we made certain to consider their provenance and there are no restrictions on the use of the public data. All the annotations were conducted and carefully reviewed by the authors. As a result, and given the fact that the datasets contain forms without any personally identifiable data, we have relative confidence that the datasets are ethically sourced.

References

Milan Aggarwal, Hiresh Gupta, Mausoom Sarkar, and Balaji Krishnamurthy. 2020. Form2seq: A framework for higher-order form structure extraction. In *EMNLP*.

Laura Chiticariu, Yunyao Li, and Frederick R. Reiss. 2013. Rule-based information extraction is dead! long live rule-based information extraction systems! In *EMNLP*.

Timo I Denk and Christian Reisswig. 2019. Bertgrid: Contextualized embedding for 2d document representation and understanding. *NeurIPS Workshop*.

Jacob Devlin, Ming-Wei Chang, Kenton Lee, and Kristina Toutanova. 2019. Bert: Pre-training of deep bidirectional transformers for language understanding. *NAACL*.

Martin Ester, Hans-Peter Kriegel, Jörg Sander, Xiaowei Xu, et al. 1996. A density-based algorithm for discovering clusters in large spatial databases with noise. In *KDD*.

Mingfei Gao, Le Xue, Chetan Ramaiah, Chen Xing, Ran Xu, and Caiming Xiong. 2021. Value retrieval with arbitrary queries for form-like documents. *arXiv preprint arXiv:2112.07820*.

Adam W Harley, Alex Ufkes, and Konstantinos G Derpanis. 2015. Evaluation of deep convolutional nets for document image classification and retrieval. In *ICDAR*.

Zheng Huang, Kai Chen, Jianhua He, Xiang Bai, Dimosthenis Karatzas, Shijian Lu, and CV Jawahar. 2019. Icdar2019 competition on scanned receipt ocr and information extraction. In *ICDAR*.

Guillaume Jaume, Hazim Kemal Ekenel, and Jean-Philippe Thiran. 2019. Funsd: A dataset for form understanding in noisy scanned documents. In *ICDARW*.

Anoop Raveendra Katti, Christian Reisswig, Cordula Guder, Sebastian Brarda, Steffen Bickel, Johannes Höhne, and Jean Baptiste Faddoul. 2018. Chargrid: Towards understanding 2d documents. *EMNLP*.

Yinhan Liu, Myle Ott, Naman Goyal, Jingfei Du, Mandar Joshi, Danqi Chen, Omer Levy, Mike Lewis, Luke Zettlemoyer, and Veselin Stoyanov. 2019. Roberta: A robustly optimized bert pretraining approach. *arXiv preprint arXiv:1907.11692*.

Bodhisattwa Prasad Majumder, Navneet Potti, Sandeep Tata, James Bradley Wendt, Qi Zhao, and Marc Najork. 2020. Representation learning for information extraction from form-like documents. In *ACL*.

Minesh Mathew, Dimosthenis Karatzas, and CV Jawahar. 2021. Docvqa: A dataset for vqa on document images. In *WACV*.

Rasmus Berg Palm, Florian Laws, and Ole Winther. 2019. Attend, copy, parse end-to-end information extraction from documents. In *ICDAR*.

Seunghyun Park, Seung Shin, Bado Lee, Junyeop Lee, Jaeheung Surh, Minjoon Seo, and Hwalsuk Lee. 2019. Cord: A consolidated receipt dataset for post-ocr parsing.

Daniel Schuster, Klemens Muthmann, Daniel Esser, Alexander Schill, Michael Berger, Christoph Weidling, Kamil Aliyev, and Andreas Hofmeier. 2013. Intellix – end-user trained information extraction for document archiving. In *ICDAR*.

Peng Tang, Xinggang Wang, Xiang Bai, and Wenyu Liu. 2017. Multiple instance detection network with online instance classifier refinement. In *CVPR*.

Ashish Vaswani, Noam Shazeer, Niki Parmar, Jakob Uszkoreit, Llion Jones, Aidan N Gomez, Lukasz Kaiser, and Illia Polosukhin. 2017. Attention is all you need. *NeurIPS*.

Zilong Wang, Mingjie Zhan, Xuebo Liu, and Ding Liang. 2020. Docstruct: A multimodal method to extract hierarchy structure in document for general form understanding. *EMNLP*.

William E Winkler. 1990. String comparator metrics and enhanced decision rules in the fellegi-sunter model of record linkage.

Yiheng Xu, Minghao Li, Lei Cui, Shaohan Huang, Furu Wei, and Ming Zhou. 2020. Layoutlm: Pre-training of text and layout for document image understanding. In *KDD*.

Le Xue, Mingfei Gao, Zeyuan Chen, Caiming Xiong, and Ran Xu. 2021. Robustness evaluation of transformer-based form field extractors via form attacks. *arXiv preprint arXiv:2110.04413*.

A Appendix

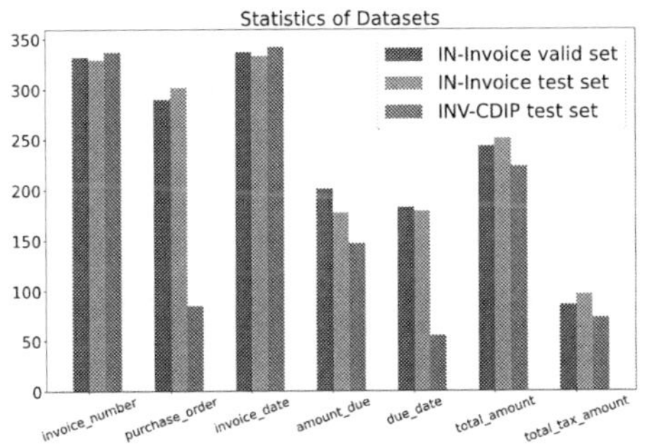

Figure A1: Field statistics of the datasets.

A.1 More Information about Datasets

The field statistics of both IN-Invoice and INV-CDIP datasets are shown in Figure A1. As we can see, the validation and test sets of our internal IN-Invoice dataset have a similar statistical distribution of fields, while the public INV-CDIP test set is different.

Moreover, the number of words per image in each dataset is shown in Figure A2. As shown, most images have 50-300 words and images with 100-150 words are typical in all the sets. We compute the number of fields per image in Figure A3. As we can see, there are averagely more fields annotated per image in IN-Invoice valid/test sets than those annotated in the INV-CDIP test set. Note that there are no field annotations in the train sets. We show the matched pseudo-labels in the train sets in Figure A3. As we can see, the number of matched pseudo-labels per image in the IN-Invoice train set is similar to that in the INV-CDIP train set.

Note that all data described was collected exclusively for the academic purpose of conducting research. The purpose of using the invoices and data was only for training and evaluating the model. No data is stored upon completion of the research process.

Field	Data Type	Key List
inv_number	number	["invoice number", "invoice #", "invoice", "invoice no.", "invoice no"]
po_number	number	["po #", "po number", "p.o. #", "p.o. number", "po", "purchase order number"]
inv_date	date	["date", "invoice date:", "invoice date"]
due_date	date	["due date"]
total_amount	number/money	["total", "invoice total"]
due_amount	number/money	["amount due", "balance due"]
total_tax	number/money	["tax"]

Table A1: Key list and data type used in our experiments.

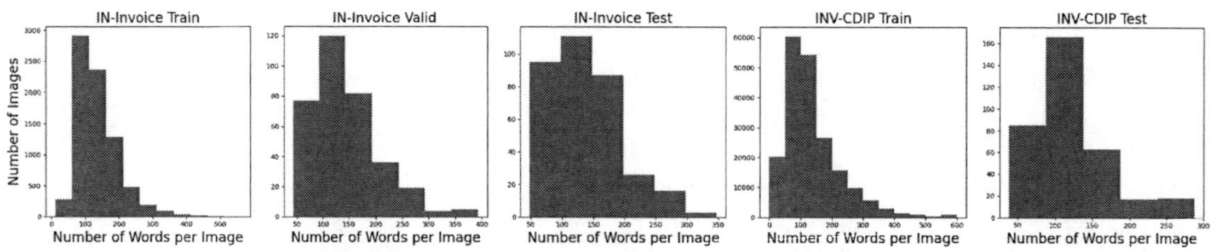

Figure A2: Number of words per image of the datasets.

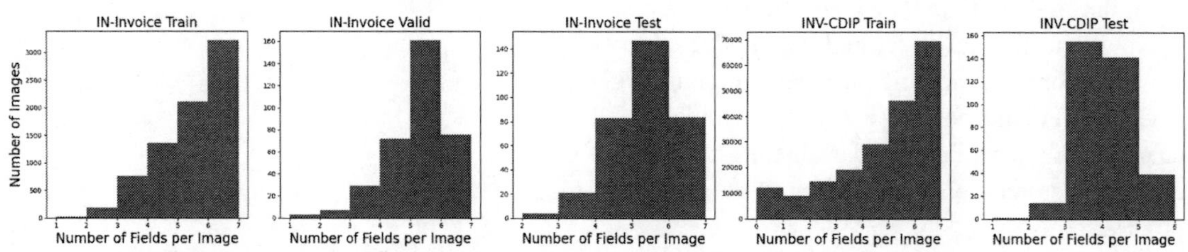

Figure A3: Number of fields per image of the datasets.

Knowledge Base Index Compression via Dimensionality and Precision Reduction

Vilém Zouhar, **Marius Mosbach**, **Miaoran Zhang** and **Dietrich Klakow**
Department of Language Science & Technology, Saarland Informatics Campus,
Saarland University, Germany
{vzouhar,mmosbach,mzhang,dklakow}@lsv.uni-saarland.de

Abstract

Recently neural network based approaches to knowledge-intensive NLP tasks, such as question answering, started to rely heavily on the combination of neural retrievers and readers. Retrieval is typically performed over a large textual knowledge base (KB) which requires significant memory and compute resources, especially when scaled up. On HotpotQA we systematically investigate reducing the size of the KB index by means of dimensionality (sparse random projections, PCA, autoencoders) and numerical precision reduction.

Our results show that PCA is an easy solution that requires very little data and is only slightly worse than autoencoders, which are less stable. All methods are sensitive to pre- and post-processing and data should always be centered and normalized both before and after dimension reduction. Finally, we show that it is possible to combine PCA with using 1bit per dimension. Overall we achieve (1) 100× compression with 75%, and (2) 24× compression with 92% original retrieval performance.

1 Introduction

Recent approaches to knowledge-intensive NLP tasks combine neural network based models with a retrieval component that leverages dense vector representations (Guu et al., 2020; Lewis et al., 2020; Petroni et al., 2021). The most straightforward example is question answering, where the retriever receives as input a question and returns relevant documents to be used by the reader (both encoder and decoder), which outputs the answer (Chen, 2020). The same approach can also be applied in other contexts, such as fact-checking (Tchechmedjiev et al., 2019) or knowledgable dialogue (Dinan et al., 2018). Moreover, this paradigm can also be applied to systems that utilize e.g. caching of contexts from the training corpus to provide better output, such as the k-nearest neighbours language model proposed by Khandelwal et al. (2019) or the dynamic gating language model mechanism by Yogatama et al. (2021). All these pipelines are generalized as retrieving an artefact from a knowledge base (Zouhar et al., 2021) on which the reader is conditioned together with the query.

Crucially, all of the previous examples rely on the quality of the retrieval component and the knowledge base. The knowledge base is usually indexed by dense vector representations[1] and the retrieval component performs maximum similarity search, commonly using the inner product or the L^2 distance, to retrieve documents[2] from the knowledge base. Only the index alone takes up a large amount of size of the knowledge base, making deployment and experimentation very difficult. The retrieval speed is also dependent on the dimensionality of the index vector. An example of a large knowledge base is the work of Borgeaud et al. (2021) which performs retrieval over a database of 1.8 billion documents.

This paper focuses on the issue of compressing the index through dimensionality and precision reduction and makes the following contributions:

- Comparison of various unsupervised index compression methods for retrieval, including random projections, PCA, autoencoder, precision reduction and their combination.
- Examination of effective pre- and post-processing transformations, showing that centering and normalization are necessary for boosting the performance.
- Analysis on the impact of adding irrelevant documents and retrieval errors. Recommendations for use by practicioners.

In Section 3, we describe the problem scenario and the experimental setup. We discuss the results

[1] Sparse representations via BM25 (Robertson et al., 1995) are also commonly used but not the focus of this work.

[2] We refer to the retrieved objects as documents though they commonly range from spans of text (e.g. 100 tokens) to the full documents.

Proceedings of the 1st Workshop on Semiparametric Methods in NLP: Decoupling Logic from Knowledge, pages 41 - 53
May 27, 2022 ©2022 Association for Computational Linguistics

of different compression methods in Section 4. We provide further analysis in Section 5 and conclude with usage recommendations in Section 6. The repository for this project is available open-source.[3]

2 Related Work

Reducing index size. A thorough overview of the issue of dimensionality reduction in information retrieval in the context of dual encoders has been done by Luan et al. (2021). Though in-depth and grounded in formal arguments, their study is focused on the limits and properties of dimension reduction in general (even with sparse representations) and the effect of document length on performance. In contrast to their work, this paper aims to compare more methods and give practical advice with experimental evidence.

A baseline for dimensionality reduction has been recently proposed by Izacard et al. (2020) in which they perform the reduction while training the document (and query) encoder by adding a low dimensional linear projection layer as the final output layer. Compared to our work, their approach is supervised.

In the concurrent work of Ma et al. (2021), PCA is also used to reduce the size of the document index. Compared to our work, they perform PCA using the combination of all question and document vectors. We show in Figures 4 and 6 that this is not needed and the PCA transformation matrix can be estimated much more efficiently. Moreover, we use different unsupervised compression approaches for comparison and perform additional analysis of our findings.

An orthogonal approach to the issue of memory cost has been proposed by Yamada et al. (2021). Instead of moving to another continuous vector representation, their proposed method maps original vectors to vectors of binary values which are trained using the signal from the downstream task. The pipeline, however, still relies on re-ranking using the uncompressed vectors. This method is different from ours and in Section 4.4 we show that they can be combined.

Finally, He et al. (2021) investigate filtering and k-means pruning for the task of kNN language modelling. This work also circumvents the issue of having to always perform an expensive retrieval of a large data store by determining whether the retrieval is actually needed for a given input.

[3]Link will be available in the camera-ready version.

Effect of normalization. Timkey and van Schijndel (2021) examine how dominating embedding dimensions can worsen retrieval performance. They study the contribution of individual dimensions find that normalization is key for document retrieval based on dense vector representation when BERT-based embeddings are used. Compared to our work, they study pre-trained BERT directly, while we focus on DPR.

3 Setup

3.1 Problem Statement and Evaluation

Given a query q, the following set of equations summarizes the conceptual progression from retrieving top k relevant documents $Z = \{d_1, d_2, \ldots, d_k\}$ from a large collection of documents $\mathcal{D}$ so that the relevance of d with q is maximized. For this, the query and the document embedding functions $f_Q : \mathcal{Q} \to \mathbb{R}^d$ and $f_D : \mathcal{D} \to \mathbb{R}^d$ are used to map the query and *all* documents to a shared embedding space and a similarity function $\text{sim} : \mathbb{R}^d \times \mathbb{R}^d \to \mathbb{R}$ approximates the relevance between query and documents. Here, we consider either the inner product or the L^2 distance as sim.[4] Finally, to speed up the similarity computation over a large set of documents and to decrease memory usage (f_D is usually precomputed), we apply **dimension reduction functions** $r_Q : \mathbb{R}^d \to \mathbb{R}^{d'}$ and $r_D : \mathbb{R}^d \to \mathbb{R}^{d'}$ for the query and document embeddings respectively. Formally, we are solving the following problem:

$$Z = \underset{d \in \mathcal{D}}{\arg\,\text{top-k}}\ \text{rel.}(q, d)\ , \text{with} \quad (1)$$

$$\text{rel.}(q, d) \approx \text{sim}(f_{\text{Q}}(q), f_{\text{D}}(d)) \quad (2)$$

$$\approx \text{sim}(r_{\text{Q}}(f_{\text{Q}}(q)), r_{\text{D}}(f_{\text{D}}(d))) \quad (3)$$

The approximation in (2) was shown to work well in practice for inner product and L^2 distance (Lin, 2021). In this case, f_Q is commonly fine-tuned for a specific downstream task. For this reason, it is desirable in (3) for the functions r_Q and r_D to be differentiable so that they can propagate the signal. These dimension-reducing functions need not be the same because even though they project to a shared vector space, the input distribution may still be different. Similarly to the query and document embedding functions, they can be fine-tuned.

[4]Cosine similarity could also be used but for computation reasons we skip it. Results are the same as for inner product and L^2 distance when the vectors are normalized.

Task Agnostic Representation. When dealing with multiple downstream tasks that share a single (large) knowledge base, typically only f_Q is fine-tuned for a specific task while f_D remains fixed (Lewis et al., 2020; Petroni et al., 2021). This assumes that the organization of the document vector space is sufficient across tasks and that only the mapping of the queries to this space needs to be trained.[5] Hence, this work is motivated primarily by finding a good r_D (because of the dominant size of the document index), though we note that r_Q is equally important and necessary because even without any vector semantics, the key and the document embeddings must have the same dimensionality.

R-Precision. To evaluate retrieval performance we compute *R-Precision* averaged over queries: (relevant documents among top k passages in $Z)/r$, k = number of passages in relevant documents, in the same way as Petroni et al. (2021). Following previous work, we consider the inner product (IP) and the L^2 distance as the similarity function.

3.2 Data

As knowledge base we use documents from English Wikipedia and follow the setup described by Petroni et al. (2021). We mark spans (original articles split into 100 token pieces, 50 million in total) as relevant for a query if they come from the same Wikipedia article as one of the provenances.[6] In order to make our experiments computationally feasible and easy to reproduce we experiment with a modified version of this knowledge base where we keep only spans of documents that are relevant to at least one query from the training or validation set of our downstream tasks. As downstream tasks, we use HotpotQA (Yang et al., 2018) for all main experiments and Natural Questions (Kwiatkowski et al., 2019) to verify that the results transfer to other datasets as well. This leads to over 2 million encoded spans for HotpotQA (see Table 6 for dataset sizes). The 768-dimensional embeddings (32-bit floats) of this dataset (both queries and documents) add up to 7GB (146GB for the whole unpruned dataset).

3.3 Uncompressed Retrieval Peformance

To establish baselines for uncompressed performance we use models based on BERT (Devlin et al., 2019). We consider (1) vanilla BERT, (2) Sentence-BERT (Reimers and Gurevych, 2019) and (3) DPR (Karpukhin et al., 2020), which was specifically trained for document retrieval. To obtain document embeddings, we use either the last hidden state representation at `[CLS]` or the average across tokens of the last layer.

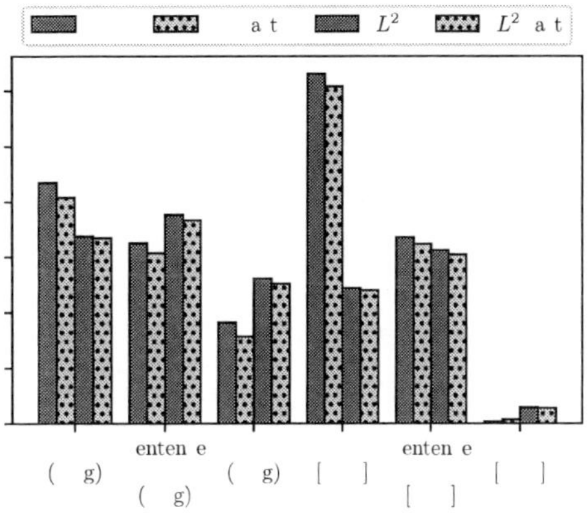

Figure 1: Comparison of different BERT-based embedding models and versions when using faster but slightly inaccurate nearest neighbour search. **[CLS]** is the specific token embedding from the last layer while **(Avg)** is all token average.

Our first experiment compares the retrieval performance of the different models on HotpotQA. The result is shown in Figure 1. In alignment with previous works (Reimers and Gurevych, 2019) an immediately noticeable conclusion is that vanilla BERT has a poor performance, especially when taking the hidden state representation for the `[CLS]` token. Next, to make computation tractable, we repeat the experiment using FAISS (Johnson et al., 2019).[7] We find that the performance loss across models is systematic, which warrants the use of this approximate nearest neighbour search for comparisons and all our following experiments will use FAISS on the DPR-CLS model.

Pre-processing Transformations. Figure 1 also shows that model performance, especially for DPR, depends heavily on what similarity metric is used for retrieval. This is because none of the models produces normalized vectors by default.

Figure 2 shows that performing only normalization ($\frac{\boldsymbol{x}}{||\boldsymbol{x}||}$) sometimes hurts the performance but when joined with centering beforehand ($\frac{\boldsymbol{x}-\bar{\boldsymbol{x}}}{||\boldsymbol{x}-\bar{\boldsymbol{x}}||}$), it improves the results (compared to no pre-

[5] Guu et al. (2020) provide evidence that this assumption can lead to worse results in some cases.

[6] Spans of the original text which help in answering the query.

[7] IndexIVFFlat, nlist=200, nprobe=100.

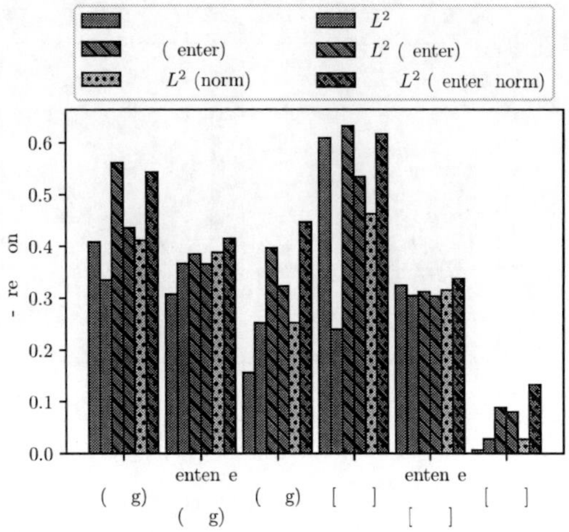

Figure 2: Effect of data centering and normalization on performance (evaluated with FAISS).

processing) in all cases. The normalization and centering is done for queries and documents separatedly. Moreover, if the vectors are normalized, then the retrieved documents are the same for L^2 and inner product. [8]

Nevertheless, we argue it still makes sense to study the compression capabilities of L^2 and the inner product separately, since the output of the compression of normalized vectors need not be normalized.

4 Compression Methods

Having established the retrieval performance of the uncompressed baseline, we now turn to methods for compressing the dense document index and the queries.

Note that we consider unsupervised methods on already trained index, for maximum ease of use and applicability. This is in contrast to supervised methods, which have access to the query-doc relevancy mapping, or to in-training dimension reduction (i.e. lower final layer dimension).

4.1 Random Projection

The simplest way to perform dimension reduction for a given index $\boldsymbol{x} \in \mathbb{R}^d$ is to randomly preserve only certain d' dimensions and drop all other dimensions:

$$f_{\text{drop.}}(\boldsymbol{x}) = (x_{m_1}, x_{m_2}, \ldots, x_{m_{d'}})$$

[8] $\arg\max_k -||\boldsymbol{a}-\boldsymbol{b}||^2 = \arg\max_k -\langle \boldsymbol{a}, \boldsymbol{a}\rangle^2 - \langle \boldsymbol{b}, \boldsymbol{b}\rangle^2 + 2\cdot\langle \boldsymbol{a}, \boldsymbol{b}\rangle = \arg\max_k 2\cdot\langle \boldsymbol{a}, \boldsymbol{b}\rangle - 2 = \arg\max_k \langle \boldsymbol{a}, \boldsymbol{b}\rangle$

Another approach is to greedily search which dimensions to drop (those that, when omitted, either improve the performance or lessen it the least):

$$p_i(\boldsymbol{x}) = (x_0, x_1, \ldots, x_{i-1}, x_{i+1}, \ldots, x_{768})$$
$$\mathcal{L}_i = \text{R-Prec}(p_i(Q), p_i(D))$$
$$m = \text{sort}_{\mathcal{L}}^{\text{desc.}}([1 \ldots 768])$$
$$f_{\text{greedy drop.}}(\boldsymbol{x}) = (x_{m_1}, x_{m_2}, \ldots, x_{m_{d'}})$$

The advantage of these two approaches is that they can be represented easily by a single $\mathbb{R}^{768\times d}$ matrix. We consider two other standard random projection methods: Gaussian random projection and Sparse random projection (Fodor, 2002). Such random projections are suitable mostly for inner product (Kaski, 1998) though the differences are removed by normalizing the vectors (which also improves the performance).

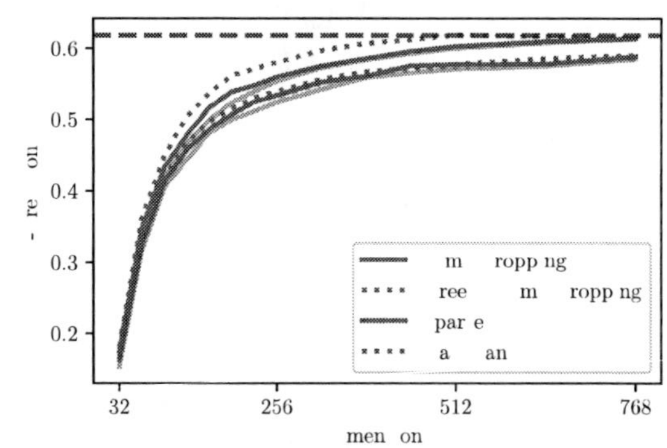

Figure 3: Dimension reduction using different random projections methods. Presented values are the max of 3 runs (except for greedy dimension dropping, which is deterministic), semi-transparent lines correspond to the minimum. Embeddings are provided by centered and normalized DPR-CLS. Final vectors are also post-processed by centering and normalization.

Results. The results of all random projection methods are shown in Figure 3. Gaussian random projection seems to perform equally to sparse random projection. The performance is not fully recovered for the two methods. Interestingly, simply dropping random dimensions led to better performance than that of sparse or Gaussian random projection. The greedy dimension dropping even improves the performance slightly over random dimension dropping in some cases before saturating and is deterministic. As shown in Table 2, the greedy dimension dropping with post-processing achieves the best performance among all random projection methods. Without post-processing, L_2 distance works better compared to inner product.

4.2 Principal Component Analysis

Another natural candidate for dimensionality reduction is principal component analysis (PCA) (F.R.S., 1901). PCA considers the dimensions with the highest variance and omits the rest. This leads to a projection matrix that projects the original data onto the principal components using an orthonormal basis T. The following loss is minimized $\mathcal{L} = \text{MSE}(\mathbf{T}'\mathbf{T}\boldsymbol{x}, \boldsymbol{x})$. Note that we fit PCA on the covariance matrix of either the document index, query embeddings or both and the trained dimension-reducing projection is then applied to both the document and query embeddings.

Results. The results of performing PCA are shown in Figure 4. First, we find that the uncompressed performance, as well as the effect of compression, is highly dependent on the data pre-processing. This should not be surprising as the PCA algorithm assumes centered and preprocessed data. Nevertheless, we stress and demonstrate the importance of this step. This is given by the normalization of the input vectors and also that the column vectors of PCA are orthonormal.

Second, when the data is not centered, the PCA is sensitive to what it is trained on. Figure 4 show systematically that training on the set of available queries provides better performance than training on the documents or a combination of both. Subsequently, after centering the data, it does not matter anymore what is used for fitting: **both the queries and the documents provide good estimates of the data variance** and the dependency on training data size for PCA is explored explicitly in Section 5.1. The reason why queries provide better results without centering is that they are more centered in the first place, as shown in Table 1.

	Avg. L^1 (std)	Avg. L^2 (std)
Documents	243.0 (20.1)	12.3 (0.6)
Queries	137.0 (7.5)	9.3 (0.2)

Table 1: Average L^1 and L^2 norms of document and query embeddings from DPR-CLS without preprocessing.

In all cases, the PCA performance starts to plateau around 128 dimensions and is within 95% of the uncompressed performance. Finally, we note that while PCA is concerned with minimizing reconstruction loss, Figure 4 shows that even after vastly decreasing the reconstruction loss, no significant improvements in retrieval performance are achieved. We further discuss this finding in Section 5.4.

Component Scaling. One potential issue of PCA is that there may be dimensions that dominate the vector space. Mu et al. (2017) suggest to simply remove the dimension corresponding to the highest eigenvalue though we find that simply scaling down the top k eigenvectors systematically outperforms standard PCA. For simplicity, we focused on the top 5 eigenvectors and performed a small-scale grid-search of the scaling factors. The best performing one was $(0.5, 0.8, 0.8, 0.9, 0.8)$ and Table 2 shows that it provides a small additional boost in retrieval performance.

4.3 Autoencoder

A straightforward extension of PCA for dimensionality reducing is to use autoencoders, which has been widely explored (Hu et al., 2014; Wang et al., 2016). Usually, the model is described by an encoder $e : \mathbb{R}^d \rightarrow \mathbb{R}^b$, a function from a higher dimension to the target (bottleneck) dimension and a decoder $r : \mathbb{R}^b \rightarrow \mathbb{R}^d$, which maps back from the target dimension to the original vector space. The final (reconstruction) loss is then commonly computed as $\mathcal{L} = \text{MSE}((r \circ e)(\boldsymbol{x}), \boldsymbol{x})$. To reduce the dimensionality of a dataset, only the function e is applied to both the query and the document embedding. We consider three models with the bottleneck:

1. A linear projection similar to PCA but without the restriction of orthonormal columns:
$$e_1(\boldsymbol{x}) = L_{128}^{768}$$
$$r_1(\boldsymbol{x}) = L_{768}^{128}$$
2. A multi-layer feed forward neural network with tanh activation:
$$e_2(\boldsymbol{x}) = L_{512}^{768} \circ \tanh \circ L_{256}^{512} \circ \tanh \circ L_{128}^{256}$$
$$r_2(\boldsymbol{x}) = L_{256}^{128} \circ \tanh \circ L_{512}^{256} \circ \tanh \circ L_{768}^{512}$$
3. The same encoder as in the previous model but with a shallow decoder:
$$e_3(\boldsymbol{x}) = L_{512}^{768} \circ \tanh \circ L_{256}^{512} \circ \tanh \circ L_{128}^{256}$$
$$r_3(\boldsymbol{x}) = L_{768}^{128}$$

Compared to PCA, it is able to model non-pairwise interaction between dimensions (in case of models 2 and 3 also non-linear interaction).

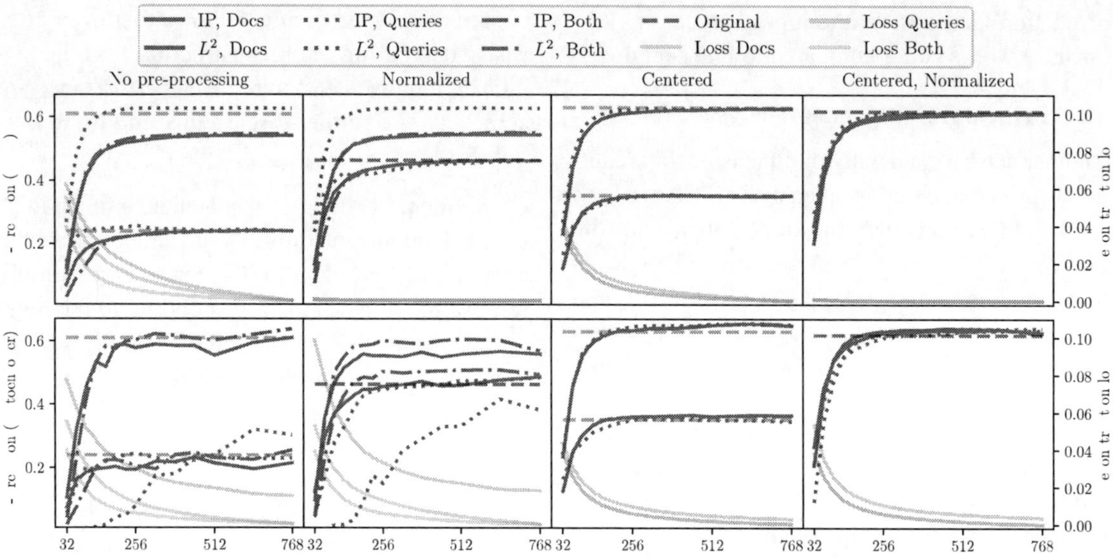

Figure 4: Dimension reduction using PCA (top) and Autoencoder (bottom) trained either on document index, query embeddings or both. Each figure corresponds to one of the four possible combinations of centering and normalizing the input data. The output vectors are not post-processed. Reconstruction loss (MSE, average for both documents and queries) is shown in transparent colour and computed in original data space. Horizontal lines show uncompressed performance. Embeddings are provided by DPR-CLS.

Results. We explore the effects of training data and pre-processing with results for the first model shown in Figure 4. Surprisingly, the Autoencoder is even more sensitive to proper pre-processing than PCA, most importantly centering which makes the results much more stable.

The rationale for the third model is that we would like the hidden representation to require as little post-processing as possible to become the original vector again. The higher performance of the model with shallow decoder, shown in Table 2 supports this reasoning. An alternative way to reduce the computation (modelling dimension relationships) in the decoder is to regularize the weights in the decoder. We make use of L_1 regularization explicitly because L_2 regularization is conceptually already present in Adam's weight decay. This improves each of the three models.

Similarly to the other reconstruction loss-based method (PCA), without post-processing, inner product works yields better results.

4.4 Precision Reduction

Lastly, we also experiment with reducing index size by lowering the float precision from 32 bits to 16 and 8 bits. Note that despite their quite high retrieval performance, they only reduce the size by 2 and 4 respectively (as opposed to 6 by dimension reduction via PCA to 128 dimensions). Another drawback is that retrieval time is not affected because the dimensionality remains the same.

Using only one bit per dimension is a special case of precision reduction suggested by Yamada et al. (2021). Because we use centered data, we can define the element-wise transformation function as:

$$f_\alpha(x_i) = \begin{cases} 1-\alpha & x_i \geq 0 \\ 0-\alpha & x_i < 0 \end{cases}$$

Bit 1 would then correspond to $1-\alpha$ and 0 to $0-\alpha$. While Yamada et al. (2021) use values 1 and 0, we work with 0.5 and -0.5 in order to be able to distinguish between certain cases when using IP-based similarity.[9] As shown in Table 2, this indeed yields a slight improvement. When applying post-processing, however, the two approaches are equivalent. While this method achieves extreme 32x compression on the disk and retains most of the retrieval performance, the downside is that if one wishes to use standard retrieval pipelines, these variables would have to be converted to a supported, larger, data type.[10]

[9] When using 0 and 1, the IP similarity of 0 and 1 is the same as 0 and 0 while for -0.5 and 0.5 they are -0.25 and 0.25 respectively.

[10] The Tevatron toolkit (Gao et al., 2022) supports mixed precision training with 16-bit floats.

Method	Compression	Original		Center + Norm.
		IP	L^2	{IP, L^2} (% original)
Original	1×	0.609	0.240	0.618 (100%)
Gaussian Projection (128)	6×	0.413	0.453	0.468 (76%)
Sparse Projection (128)	6×	0.398	0.448	0.457 (74%)
Dimension Dropping (128)	6×	0.426	0.466	0.478 (77%)
Greedy Dimension Dropping (128)	6×	0.447	0.478	0.504 (82%)
PCA (128)	6×	0.577	0.562	0.579 (94%)
PCA (128, scaled top 5)	6×	0.586	0.572	0.592 (96%)
Autoencoder (128, single layer)	6×	0.585	0.569	0.588 (95%)
Autoencoder (128, full)	6×	0.564	0.560	0.588 (95%)
Autoencoder (128, shallow decoder)	6×	0.599	0.582	0.599 (97%)
Autoencoder (128, single layer) + L_1	6×	0.600	0.587	0.601 (97%)
Autoencoder (128, full) + L_1	6×	0.573	0.569	0.589 (95%)
Autoencoder (128, shallow decoder) + L_1	6×	0.601	0.591	0.601 (97%)
Precision 16-bit	2×	0.612	0.610	0.615 (100%)
Precision 8-bit	4×	0.613	0.610	0.614 (99%)
Precision 1-bit (offset 0.5)	32×	0.559	0.556	0.561 (91%)
Precision 1-bit (offset 0)	32×	0.530	0.556	0.561 (91%)
PCA (245) + Precision 1-bit (offset 0.5)	100×	0.459	0.458	0.461 (75%)
PCA (128) + Precision 8-bit	24×	0.558	0.553	0.567 (92%)

Table 2: Overview of compression method performance (from 768) using either L^2 or inner product for retrieval. Inputs are based on centered and normalized output of DPR-CLS and the outputs optionally post-processed again. Performance is measured by R-Precision on HotpotQA.

4.5 Combination of PCA and Precision Reduction

Finally, reducing precision can be readily combined with dimension reduction methods, such as PCA (prior to changing the data type). The results in Figure 5 show that PCA can be combined with e.g. 8-bit precision reduction with negligible loss in performance. As shown in the last row of Table 2, this can lead to the compressed size be 100x smaller while retaining 75% retrieval performance on HotpotQA and 89% for NaturalQuestions (see Table 7).

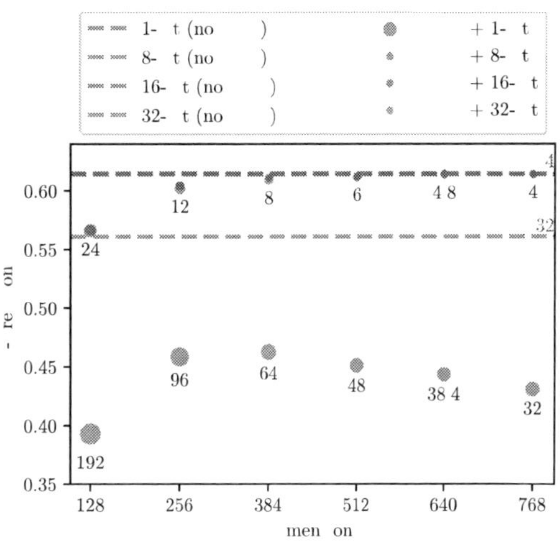

Figure 5: Combination of PCA and precision reduction. Compression ratio is shown in text. 16-bit and 32-bit values overlap with 8-bit and their compression ratios are not shown. Measured on HotpotQA with DPR-CLS.

5 Analysis

5.1 Model Comparison

The comparison of all discussed dimension reduction methods is shown in Table 2. It also shows the role of centering and normalization post-encoding which systematically improves the performance. The best performing model for dimension reduction is the autoencoder with L_1 regularization and either just a single projection layer for the encoder and decoder or with the shallow decoder (6x compression with 97% retrieval performance). Additionally, Appendix B compares training and evaluation speeds of common implementations.

5.2 Data size

A crucial aspect of the PCA and autoencoder methods is how much data they need for training. In the following, we experimented with limiting the number of training samples for PCA and the linear autoencoder. Results are shown in Figure 6.

While Ma et al. (2021) used a much larger training set to fit PCA, we find that PCA requires very

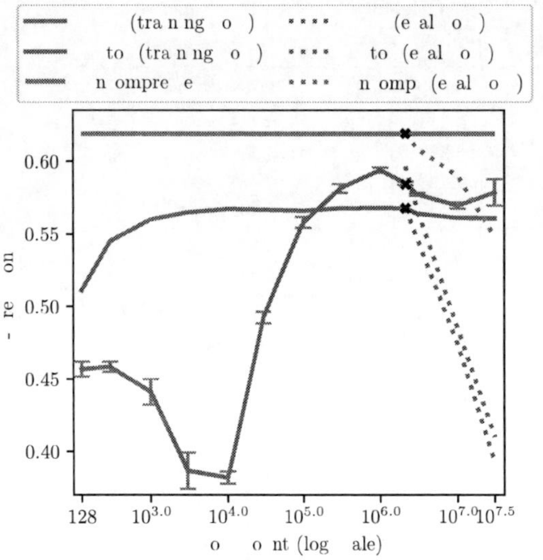

Figure 6: Dependency of PCA and autoencoder performance (evaluated on HotpotQA dev data, trained on document encodings, pre- and post-processing) by modifying the training data (solid lines) and by adding irrelevant documents to the retrieval pool (dashed lines). Black crosses indicate the original training size. Vertical bars are 95% confidence intervals using t-distibution (across 6 runs with random model initialization and sampling). Note the log scale on the x-axis and the truncation of the y-axis.

few samples (lower-bounded by 128 which is also the number of dimensions used for this experiment). This is because in the case of PCA training data is used to estimate the data covariance matrix which has been shown to work well when using a few samples (Tadjudin and Landgrebe, 1999). Additionally, we find that overall the autoencoder needs more data to outperform PCA.

Next, we experimented with adding more (potentially irrelevant) documents to the knowledge base. For this, we kept the training data for the autoencoder and PCA to the original size. The results are shown as dashed lines in Figure 6. Retrieval performance quickly deteriorates for both models (faster than for the uncompressed case), highlighting the importance of filtering irrelevant documents from the knowledge base.

5.3 Retrieval errors

So far, our evaluation focused on quantitative comparisons. In the following, we compare the distribution of documents retrieved before and after compression to investigate if there are systematic differences. We carry out this analysis using HotpotQA which, by design, requires two documents in order to answer a given query. We compare retrieval with the original document embeddings to retrieval with PCA and 1-bit compression.

We find that there are no systematic differences compared to the uncompressed retrieval. This is demonstrated by the small off-diagonal values in Figure 7. This result shows that if the retriever working with uncompressed embeddings returns two relevant documents in the top-k for a given query, also the retriever working with the compressed index is very likely to include the same two documents in the top-k. This is further shown by the Pearson correlation in Table 4. This suggests that the compressed index can be used on downstream tasks with predictable performance loss based on the slightly worsened retrieval performance. Furthermore, there do not seem to be any systematic differences even between the two vastly different compression methods used for this experiment (PCA and 1-bit precision). This indicates that, despite their methodological differences, the two compression approaches seem to remove the same redundances in the uncompressed data. We leave a more detailed exploration of these findings for future work.

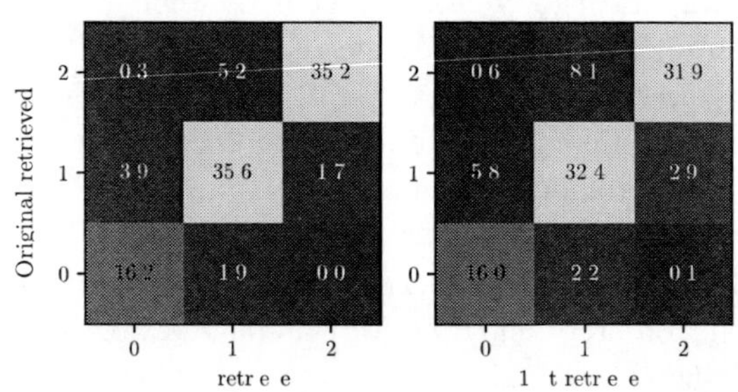

Figure 7: Distribution of the number of retrieved documents for HotpotQA queries before and after compression: PCA (128) and 1-bit precision with R-Precisions (centered & normalized) of 0.579 and 0.561, respectively.

5.4 Pitfalls of Reconstruction Loss

Despite PCA and autoencoder being the most successful methods, low reconstruction loss provides no theoretical guarantee to the retrieval performance. Consider a simple linear projection that can be represented as a diagonal matrix that projects to a space of the same dimensionality. This function has a trivial inverse and therefore no information is lost when it is applied. The retrieval is however disrupted, as it will mostly depend on the first dimension and nothing else. This is a major flaw of approaches that minimize the vector reconstruction loss because the optimized quantity is different to the actual goal.

$$R = \begin{pmatrix} 10^{99} & 0 & \cdots & 0 \\ 0 & 1 & \cdots & 0 \\ \vdots & \vdots & \ddots & \vdots \\ 0 & 0 & \cdots & 1 \end{pmatrix} \quad R^{-1} = \begin{pmatrix} 10^{-99} & 0 & \cdots & 0 \\ 0 & 1 & \cdots & 0 \\ \vdots & \vdots & \ddots & \vdots \\ 0 & 0 & \cdots & 1 \end{pmatrix}$$

Distance Learning. The task of dimensionality reduction has been explored by standard statistical methods by the name manifold learning. The most used method is t-distributed stochastic neighbor (t-SNE) embedding built on the work of Hinton and Roweis (2002) or multidimensional scaling (Kruskal, 1964; Borg and Groenen, 2005). They organize a new vector space (of lower dimensionality) so that the L^2 distances follow those of the original space (extensions to other metrics also exist). Although the optimization goal is more in line with our task of vector space compression with the preservation of nearest neighbours, methods of manifold learning are limited by the large computation costs[11] and the fact that they do not construct a function but rather move the discrete points in the new space to lower the optimization loss. This makes it not applicable for online purposes (i.e. adding new samples that need to be compressed as well).

The main disadvantage of the approaches based on reconstruction loss is that their optimization goal strays from what we are interested in, namely preserving distances between vectors. We tried to reformulate the problem in terms of deep learning and gradient-based optimization to alleviate the issue of speed and extensibility of standard manifold learning approaches. We try to learn a function that maps the original vector space to a lower-dimensional one while preserving similarities. That can be either a simple linear projection A or generally a more complex differentiable function f:

$$\mathcal{L} = \text{MSE}(\text{sim}(f(t_i), f(t_j)), \text{sim}(t_i, t_j))$$

After the function f is fitted, both the training and new data can be compressed by its application. As opposed to manifold learning which usually leverages specific properties of the metrics, here they can be any differentiable functions. The optimization was, however, too slow, underperforming (between sparse projection and PCA) and did not currently provide any benefits.

We also tried to use unsupervised contrastive learning by considering close neighbours in the original space as positive samples and distant neighbours as negative samples but reached similar results.

6 Discussion

In this section we briefly discuss the main conclusions from our experiments and analysis in the form of recommendations for NLP practicioners.

Importance of Pre-/post-processing. As our results show, for all methods (and models), centering and normalization should be done before and after dimension reduction, as it boosts the performance of every model.

Method recommendation. While most compression methods achieve similar retrieval performance and compression ratios (cf. Table 2 and Table 7), PCA stands out in the following regards: (1) It requires only minimal implementation effort and no tuning of hyper-parameters beyond selecting which principal components to keep; (2) as our analysis shows, the PCA matrix can be estimated well with only 1000 document or query embeddings. It is not necessary to learn a transformation matrix on the full knowledge base; (3) PCA can easily be combined with precision reduction based approaches.

7 Summary

In this work, we examined several simple unsupervised methods for dimensionality reduction for retrieval-based NLP tasks: random projections, PCA, autoencoder and precision reduction and their combination. We also documented the data requirements of each method and their reliance on pre- and post-processing.

Future work. As shown in prior works, dimension reduction can take place also during training where the loss is more in-line with the retrieval goal. Methods for dimension reduction after training, however, rely mostly on reconstruction loss, which is suboptimal. Therefore more research for dimension reduction methods is needed, such as fast manifold or distance-based learning.

[11]The common fast implementation for t-SNE, Barnes-Hut (Barnes and Hut, 1986; Van Der Maaten, 2013) is based on either quadtrees or octrees and is limited to 3 dimensions.

Acknowledgements

This work was funded by the Deutsche Forschungsgemeinschaft (DFG, German Research Foundation) – Project-ID 232722074 – SFB 1102. Thank you to the reviewers, Badr M. Abdullah and many others for their comments to our work.

References

Josh Barnes and Piet Hut. 1986. A hierarchical o (n log n) force-calculation algorithm. *nature*, 324(6096):446–449.

Ingwer Borg and Patrick JF Groenen. 2005. *Modern multidimensional scaling: Theory and applications*. Springer Science & Business Media.

Sebastian Borgeaud, Arthur Mensch, Jordan Hoffmann, Trevor Cai, Eliza Rutherford, Katie Millican, George van den Driessche, Jean-Baptiste Lespiau, Bogdan Damoc, Aidan Clark, Diego de Las Casas, Aurelia Guy, Jacob Menick, Roman Ring, Tom Hennigan, Saffron Huang, Loren Maggiore, Chris Jones, Albin Cassirer, Andy Brock, Michela Paganini, Geoffrey Irving, Oriol Vinyals, Simon Osindero, Karen Simonyan, Jack W. Rae, Erich Elsen, and Laurent Sifre. 2021. Improving language models by retrieving from trillions of tokens.

Charles L Chen. 2020. *Neural Network Models for Tasks in Open-Domain and Closed-Domain Question Answering*. Ohio University.

Jacob Devlin, Ming-Wei Chang, Kenton Lee, and Kristina Toutanova. 2019. Bert: Pre-training of deep bidirectional transformers for language understanding. In *Proceedings of the 2019 Conference of the North American Chapter of the Association for Computational Linguistics: Human Language Technologies, Volume 1 (Long and Short Papers)*, pages 4171–4186.

Emily Dinan, Stephen Roller, Kurt Shuster, Angela Fan, Michael Auli, and Jason Weston. 2018. Wizard of wikipedia: Knowledge-powered conversational agents. *arXiv preprint arXiv:1811.01241*.

Imola K Fodor. 2002. A survey of dimension reduction techniques. Technical report, Citeseer.

Karl Pearson F.R.S. 1901. Liii. on lines and planes of closest fit to systems of points in space. *The London, Edinburgh, and Dublin Philosophical Magazine and Journal of Science*, 2(11):559–572.

Luyu Gao, Xueguang Ma, Jimmy Lin, and Jamie Callan. 2022. Tevatron: An efficient and flexible toolkit for dense retrieval. *arXiv preprint arXiv:2203.05765*.

Kelvin Guu, Kenton Lee, Zora Tung, Panupong Pasupat, and Ming-Wei Chang. 2020. Realm: Retrieval-augmented language model pre-training. *arXiv preprint arXiv:2002.08909*.

Junxian He, Graham Neubig, and Taylor Berg-Kirkpatrick. 2021. Efficient nearest neighbor language models. In *Proceedings of the 2021 Conference on Empirical Methods in Natural Language Processing*, pages 5703–5714.

Geoffrey Hinton and Sam T Roweis. 2002. Stochastic neighbor embedding. In *NIPS*, volume 15, pages 833–840. Citeseer.

Changjie Hu, Xiaoli Hou, and Yonggang Lu. 2014. Improving the architecture of an autoencoder for dimension reduction. In *2014 IEEE 11th Intl Conf on Ubiquitous Intelligence and Computing and 2014 IEEE 11th Intl Conf on Autonomic and Trusted Computing and 2014 IEEE 14th Intl Conf on Scalable Computing and Communications and Its Associated Workshops*, pages 855–858. IEEE.

Gautier Izacard, Fabio Petroni, Lucas Hosseini, Nicola De Cao, Sebastian Riedel, and Edouard Grave. 2020. A memory efficient baseline for open domain question answering. *arXiv preprint arXiv:2012.15156*.

Jeff Johnson, Matthijs Douze, and Hervé Jégou. 2019. Billion-scale similarity search with gpus. *IEEE Transactions on Big Data*.

Vladimir Karpukhin, Barlas Oguz, Sewon Min, Patrick Lewis, Ledell Wu, Sergey Edunov, Danqi Chen, and Wen-tau Yih. 2020. Dense passage retrieval for open-domain question answering. In *Proceedings of the 2020 Conference on Empirical Methods in Natural Language Processing (EMNLP)*, pages 6769–6781.

Samuel Kaski. 1998. Dimensionality reduction by random mapping: Fast similarity computation for clustering. In *1998 IEEE International Joint Conference on Neural Networks Proceedings. IEEE World Congress on Computational Intelligence (Cat. No. 98CH36227)*, volume 1, pages 413–418. IEEE.

Urvashi Khandelwal, Omer Levy, Dan Jurafsky, Luke Zettlemoyer, and Mike Lewis. 2019. Generalization through memorization: Nearest neighbor language models. *arXiv preprint arXiv:1911.00172*.

Joseph B Kruskal. 1964. Nonmetric multidimensional scaling: a numerical method. *Psychometrika*, 29(2):115–129.

Tom Kwiatkowski, Jennimaria Palomaki, Olivia Redfield, Michael Collins, Ankur Parikh, Chris Alberti, Danielle Epstein, Illia Polosukhin, Jacob Devlin, Kenton Lee, et al. 2019. Natural questions: a benchmark for question answering research. *Transactions of the Association for Computational Linguistics*, 7:453–466.

Patrick Lewis, Ethan Perez, Aleksandra Piktus, Fabio Petroni, Vladimir Karpukhin, Naman Goyal, Heinrich Küttler, Mike Lewis, Wen-tau Yih, Tim Rocktäschel, et al. 2020. Retrieval-augmented generation for knowledge-intensive nlp tasks. *arXiv preprint arXiv:2005.11401*.

Jimmy Lin. 2021. A proposed conceptual framework for a representational approach to information retrieval. *arXiv preprint arXiv:2110.01529*.

Yi Luan, Jacob Eisenstein, Kristina Toutanova, and Michael Collins. 2021. Sparse, dense, and attentional representations for text retrieval. *Transactions of the Association for Computational Linguistics*, 9:329–345.

Xueguang Ma, Minghan Li, Kai Sun, Ji Xin, and Jimmy Lin. 2021. Simple and effective unsupervised redundancy elimination to compress dense vectors for passage retrieval. In *Proceedings of the 2021 Conference on Empirical Methods in Natural Language Processing*, pages 2854–2859.

Jiaqi Mu, Suma Bhat, and Pramod Viswanath. 2017. All-but-the-top: Simple and effective postprocessing for word representations. *arXiv preprint arXiv:1702.01417*.

Fabio Petroni, Aleksandra Piktus, Angela Fan, Patrick Lewis, Majid Yazdani, Nicola De Cao, James Thorne, Yacine Jernite, Vladimir Karpukhin, Jean Maillard, et al. 2021. Kilt: a benchmark for knowledge intensive language tasks. In *Proceedings of the 2021 Conference of the North American Chapter of the Association for Computational Linguistics: Human Language Technologies*, pages 2523–2544.

Nils Reimers and Iryna Gurevych. 2019. Sentence-bert: Sentence embeddings using siamese bert-networks. In *Proceedings of the 2019 Conference on Empirical Methods in Natural Language Processing and the 9th International Joint Conference on Natural Language Processing (EMNLP-IJCNLP)*, pages 3973–3983.

Stephen E Robertson, Steve Walker, Susan Jones, Micheline M Hancock-Beaulieu, Mike Gatford, et al. 1995. Okapi at trec-3. *Nist Special Publication Sp*, 109:109.

Saldju Tadjudin and David A Landgrebe. 1999. Covariance estimation with limited training samples. *IEEE Transactions on Geoscience and Remote Sensing*, 37(4):2113–2118.

Andon Tchechmedjiev, Pavlos Fafalios, Katarina Boland, Malo Gasquet, Matthäus Zloch, Benjamin Zapilko, Stefan Dietze, and Konstantin Todorov. 2019. Claimskg: A knowledge graph of fact-checked claims. In *International Semantic Web Conference*, pages 309–324. Springer.

William Timkey and Marten van Schijndel. 2021. All bark and no bite: Rogue dimensions in transformer language models obscure representational quality. In *Proceedings of the 2021 Conference on Empirical Methods in Natural Language Processing*, pages 4527–4546.

Laurens Van Der Maaten. 2013. Barnes-hut-sne. *arXiv preprint arXiv:1301.3342*.

Yasi Wang, Hongxun Yao, and Sicheng Zhao. 2016. Auto-encoder based dimensionality reduction. *Neurocomputing*, 184:232–242.

Ikuya Yamada, Akari Asai, and Hannaneh Hajishirzi. 2021. Efficient passage retrieval with hashing for open-domain question answering. *arXiv preprint arXiv:2106.00882*.

Zhilin Yang, Peng Qi, Saizheng Zhang, Yoshua Bengio, William Cohen, Ruslan Salakhutdinov, and Christopher D Manning. 2018. Hotpotqa: A dataset for diverse, explainable multi-hop question answering. In *Proceedings of the 2018 Conference on Empirical Methods in Natural Language Processing*, pages 2369–2380.

Dani Yogatama, Cyprien de Masson d'Autume, and Lingpeng Kong. 2021. Adaptive semiparametric language models. *Transactions of the Association for Computational Linguistics*, 9:362–373.

Vilém Zouhar, Marius Mosbach, Debanjali Biswas, and Dietrich Klakow. 2021. Artefact retrieval: Overview of NLP models with knowledge base access. In *Workshop on Commonsense Reasoning and Knowledge Bases*.

Hyperparameters	
Batch size	128
Optimizer	Adam
Learning rate	10^{-3}
L_1 regularization	$10^{-5.9}$

Table 3: Hyperparameters of autoencoder architectures described in Section 4.3. L_1 regularization is used only when explicitly mentioned.

A Pre-processing

Another common approach before any feature selection is to use z-scores ($\frac{x-\bar{x}}{\sigma}$) instead of the original values. Its boost in performance is however similar to that of centering and normalization. The effects of each pre-processing step are in Table 5. The significant differences in performance show the importance of data pre-processing (agnostic to model selection).

B Speed

Despite the autoencoder providing slightly better retrieval performance and PCA being generally easier to use (due to the lack of hyperparameters), there are several tradeoffs in model selection. Once the models are trained, the runtime performance (encoding) is comparable though for PCA it is a single matrix projection while for the autoencoder it may be several layers and activation functions.

Depending on the specific library used for implementation, however, the results differ. Figure 8 shows that the autoencoder (implemented in PyTorch) is much slower than any other model when run on a CPU but the fastest when run on a GPU. Similarly, PCA works best if used from the PyTorch library (whether on CPU or GPU) and from the standard Scikit package. Except for Scikit, there seems to be little relation between the target dimensionality and computation time.

[12]PyTorch 1.9.1, scikit-learn 0.23.2, RTX 2080 Ti (CUDA 11.4), 64×2.1GHz Intel Xeon E5-2683 v4, 1TB RAM.

	Uncompressed	PCA	1bit
Uncompressed	1.00		
PCA	0.87	1.00	
1bit	0.81	0.80	1.00

Table 4: Correlation of the number of retrieved documents for HotpotQA queries in different retrieval modes: uncompressed, PCA (128) and 1-bit precision with R-Precisions (centered & normalized) of 0.618, 0.579 and 0.561, respectively.

	IP	L^2
DPR-CLS	0.609	0.240
Center	0.630	0.353
Z-Score	0.632	0.525
Norm.	0.463	
Center + norm.	0.618	
Z-Score + norm.	0.621	

Table 5: Effect of pre-processing transformations on embeddings produced by DPR-CLS. Means and standard deviations are computed separately for documents and queries. Transformation into z-scores includes centering.

Dataset	Train	Dev	Doc.
HP	69k	6k	49.7 Mio.
HP (pruned)	69k	6k	2.1 Mio.
NQ (pruned)	78k	2k	1.6 Mio.

Table 6: Number of training and dev queries and documents for HotpotQA and Natural Questions. Train and dev columns are queries.

C Comparison on Natural Questions

We also show the major experiments in Table 7 (table structure equivalent to that for the pruned dataset in Table 2) on Natural Question (Kwiatkowski et al., 2019) with identical dataset pre-processing. The performance is overall larger because the task is different and the set of documents is lower (1.5 million spans) but comparatively the trends are in line with the previous conclusions of the paper.

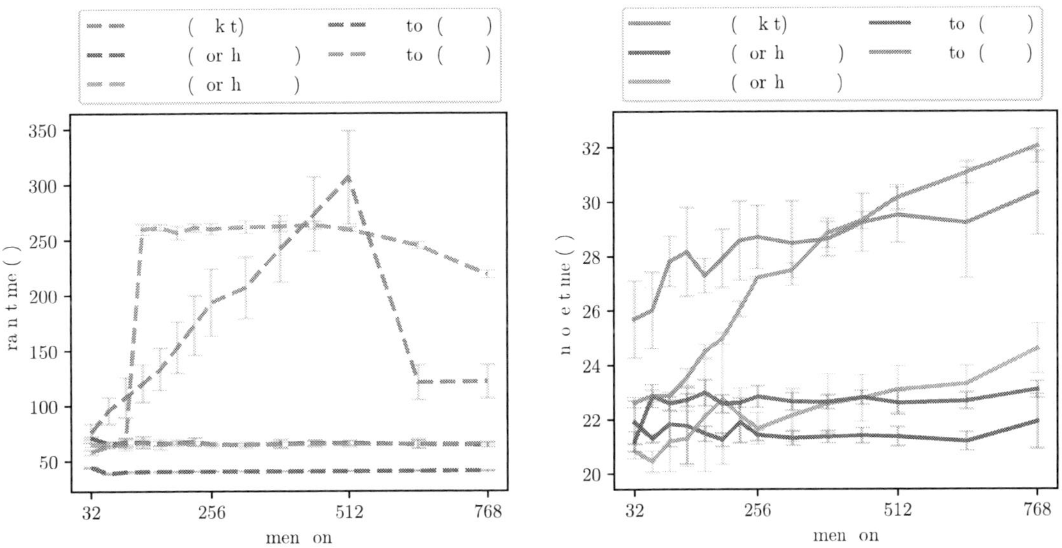

Figure 8: Speed comparison of PCA and autoencoder (model 3) implemented in PyTorch and Scikit[12] split into training and encoding parts. Models were trained on documents and queries jointly (normalized). Error bars are 95% confidence intervals using t-distribution (5 runs).

Method	**Compression**	**Original**		**Center + Norm.**
		IP	L^2	{IP, L^2} (% original)
Original	1×	0.934	0.758	0.920 (100%)
Gaussian Projection	6×	0.825	0.848	0.855 (93%)
Sparse Projection	6×	0.826	0.848	0.856 (93%)
Dimension Dropping	6×	0.840	0.863	0.867 (94%)
Greedy Dimension Dropping	6×	0.845	0.873	0.873 (95%)
PCA	6×	0.908	0.907	0.910 (99%)
PCA (scaled top 5)	6×	0.916	0.910	0.920 (100%)
Autoencoder (single layer)	6×	0.915	0.910	0.914 (99%)
Autoencoder (full)	6×	0.903	0.907	0.910 (99%)
Autoencoder (shallow decoder)	6×	0.916	0.918	0.919 (100%)
Autoencoder + L_1 (single layer)	6×	0.918	0.918	0.921 (100%)
Autoencoder + L_1 (full)	6×	0.909	0.910	0.913 (99%)
Autoencoder + L_1 (shallow decoder)	6×	0.918	0.917	0.919 (100%)
Precision 16-bit	2×	0.921	0.917	0.920 (100%)
Precision 8-bit	4×	0.920	0.921	0.922 (100%)
Precision 1-bit (offset 0.5)	32×	0.902	0.902	0.904 (98%)
Precision 1-bit (offset 0)	32×	0.892	0.902	0.904 (98%)
PCA (245) + Precision 1-bit (offset 0.5)	100×	0.854	0.862	0.858 (93%)
PCA (128) + Precision 8-bit	24×	0.906	0.904	0.909 (99%)

Table 7: Overview of compression method performance (from 768) using either L^2 or inner product for retrieval. Inputs are based on (1) original and (2) centered and normalized output of DPR-CLS. Performance is measured by R-Precision on NaturalQuestions.

Author Index

Association for Computational Linguistics
209 N. Eighth Street
Stroudsburg, Pennsylvania 18360

ISBN 978-1-7138-6752-4

9 781713 867524

CURRAN ASSOCIATES INC.
proceedings
.com

1st Workshop Towards Ethical and Inclusive Conversational AI: Language Attitudes, Linguistic Diversity, and Language Rights (TEICAI 2024)

St. Julian's, Malta
22 March 2024